"OH, HOW HARD IT IS
IN PRAYING TO REACH THE AMEN."
—SØREN KIERKEGAARD

"NOT ALL WHO WANDER ARE LOST."
—J. R. R. TOLKEIN

Creech
Ranch House

LONG WANDERING PRAYER

An Invitation to Walk with God

DAVID HANSEN

InterVarsity Press
Downers Grove, Illinois

InterVarsity Press
P.O. Box 1400, Downers Grove, IL 60515-1426
World Wide Web: www.ivpress.com
E-mail: mail@ivpress.com

InterVarsity Press® is the book-publishing division of InterVarsity Christian Fellowship/USA®, a
student movement active on campus at hundreds of universities, colleges and schools of nursing in
the United States of America, and a member movement of the International Fellowship of
Evangelical Students. For information about local and regional activities, write Public Relations
Dept., InterVarsity Christian Fellowship/USA, 6400 Schroeder Rd., P.O. Box 7895, Madison, WI
53707-7895.

All Scripture quotations, unless otherwise indicated, are taken from the New Revised Standard
Version of the Bible, copyright 1989 by the Division of Christian Education of the National Council
of the Churches of Christ in the USA. Used by permission. All rights reserved.

Cover illustration: Derek P. Redfearn/Image Bank

ISBN 0-8308-2283-6

Printed in the United States of America ∞

Library of Congress Cataloging-in-Publication Data

Hansen, David, 1953
   Long wandering prayer: an invitation to walk with God/David Hansen
     p. cm.
   Includes bibliographical references.
   ISBN 0-8308-2283-6 (alk paper)
   1 Prayer—Christianity. I. Title
   BV215.H345 2001
   248.3'2—dc21

                                        00-047167

20	19	18	17	16	15	14	13	12	11	10	9	8	7	6	5	4	3	2	1
17	16	15	14	13	12	11	10	09	08	07	06	05	04	03	02	01			

For Mike,
who asked the questions
that made this book possible,
and who will remain unconvinced
by its answers.

Acknowledgments

I am deeply grateful to InterVarsity Press for its continued support of my writing projects. Special thanks go to Rodney Clapp who helped me start the book and Cindy Bunch-Hotaling who helped me finish it. I thank IVP for sending out the first draft to two anonymous readers/evaluators. I learned as much from the reader who disliked the book as I did from the reader who liked it. I am grateful to friends who read the manuscript and made many helpful comments: Debbie Hansen, Tim Fearer, John Gilmore and Dave Dooley. Cindy Bunch-Hotaling's critique and encouragement was extremely helpful.

As I will explain in "Orientation to Wandering," I have included prayer narratives from friends in Christ who have prayed long wandering prayers for years. Their contributions to this book are immense. Naturally, they are not responsible for what I say in this book. I list them in alphabetical order: Doreen Clark, Mike Coughlin, Jan Peterson, Lynne Rienstra and Steve Trotter.

I thank the members of the Belgrade Community Church and Kenwood Baptist Church. Both churches have been exceedingly kind and supportive of my long and tiring writing projects. They have truly borne the burden lightly. The difficulties I have caused my churches far exceed any examples I cite of difficulties in pastoral ministry due to my intractable faults as a pastor and as a Christian.

I cannot begin to thank Debbie, Evan, Sarah and Laura adequately for their unfailingly gracious acceptance of the heavy weight of sharing life with a pastor who is also a writer.

Orientation to Wandering

Long wandering prayer happens on the inside like it happens on the outside. It is mental wandering in the presence of God, corresponding to physical wandering in the presence of God. Long wandering prayer involves leaving our normal environment for the express purpose of spending many hours alone with God. It involves walking, or at least moving, and stopping whenever we want, to consider a lily for as long as we desire. Long wandering prayer uses the fact that our minds wander as an advantage to prayer rather than as a disadvantage. In long wandering prayer we recognize that what we want to pray about may not be what God wants us pray about. Our obsessive drive to control our minds in the presence of God, that is, to pray about one thing or stick to one list, may be a form of hiding from God. In this kind of prayer we recognize the wandering mind as a precious resource for complex and startling dialogue with God.

I have prayed long wandering prayers for thirty years. I am a wanderer by nature. As a child and as an adolescent I wandered alone in forests, fields and city streets many years before it dawned on me that I was wandering in the presence of God. Some of my earliest memories are of wandering in marshlands near our house in Minneapolis, Minnesota. I do not suppose sensible mothers today let their four-year-old boys wander alone through marshes with a popgun, hoping to shoot a duck, but my mother did, God love her. She must have been afraid for me. I suppose she imagined me stepping into a sinkhole and never returning. Nevertheless, perhaps I gave her little choice. By letting me go, at least she could tell me what to avoid and she could suggest when I return. Breaking away from others to spend time alone wandering and thinking is one of the defining characteristics of my life. Living on the outskirts of Denver, Colorado, as a grade-schooler I often walked two miles to school in a snowstorm, through fields that are now Interstate 70. I could have taken the bus. I wanted to walk alone in the storm to think. During my grade school years I walked the open fields and mesas around Denver, looking at birds and plants, collecting rocks and telling stories to myself.

We moved to Southern California the summer between my sixth-grade and seventh-grade years. I hated this because I missed Colorado. But I was changing too. I forgot the open spaces in Colorado because Southern California in the 1960s was a very fun place to be a teenager. Still, I found ways to be alone. I loved tinkering with inventions in our garage. I exploded some things, broke and lost a lot of my dad's tools, and I took apart some engines that I never got back together. I was not mechanical at all. It was just a way of being busy so I could be alone and think about other things. If I had been thinking about what I was doing, I would have started fewer fires, but my thought life would have been far less interesting.

I became a follower of Christ during high school. After this I began injecting some short prayers to my time alone thinking. It began with the feeling that God was there, even when I was alone. I felt the truth of Psalm 139 before I read it: "You know when I sit down and when I rise up; you discern my thoughts from far away" (Ps 139:2). The awareness that God was with me when I was alone became the willingness to pray when the impulse occurred. This brought my entire thinking process into the presence of God, the good thinking and the bad thinking, the logical and the illogical, the pure and the impure, the loving and the unloving. Quite early in my Christian life I ran across Paul's injunction, "Whatever is true, whatever is honorable, whatever is just, whatever is pure, whatever is pleasing, whatever is commendable, if there is any excellence and if there is anything worthy of praise, think about these things" (Phil 4:8). I couldn't always think about good things. Except later, as a Christian, through reading the Bible, going to youth group and corporate worship, I had some criteria for knowing the difference.

My first year of college I was a thousand miles from home with a low draft number and no student deferment. I was in love with a young woman, a first year student at another college, whose father had already died in the Vietnam War. I felt called to the ministry, and it scared me to death. Of course, I don't remember studying much that year. I remember walking the streets of Salem, Oregon, hour upon hour, through dreary winter rains, talking to God. Much of my adult life pivoted on decisions made in those long wandering prayers. I returned to Southern California to finish college.

My junior and senior year of college I worked in my church running a junior high group of about seventy-five kids. My style of ministry must have seemed odd to the church staff. I wrote the Sunday school curriculum for the group. It did occur to me that professionals get paid to write junior high curriculum and that my time would have been better spent planning events and spending time with teachers and kids. Nevertheless, I felt a deep desire to write the curriculum myself, and I was too shy to spend much time with the teachers or the kids. So I skate boarded over the long concrete walks of the church, circling the campus, thinking and praying about my lesson plans, and praying for the kids and the teachers. No one at the church questioned my style because it seemed to be working and "No Skateboarding" signs were not yet invented. Twenty-five years later the retiring pastor of the church said that my two-year junior high ministry laid the groundwork for a continuously successful junior high ministry in the church. What I remember doing most is skateboarding while I thought and prayed.

At seminary in New England, I walked and prayed down maple-lined lanes. The first time I walked through a snowstorm and prayed, eleven years after leaving Colorado, I wept at the beauty. I bundled up and walked in blizzards just like when I was a kid in Colorado. I surf fished with big shiny lures I made from aluminum strips cut from beached beer cans. What fun, fishing and praying!

In January of 1983, four years after seminary, Debbie and I landed in the wilds of Montana with three little children to raise and two struggling one-hundred-year-old churches to serve. My popgun and skateboard were gone, but I had a fly rod. Not much of the land was posted back then, and I wandered the rivers and streams of Montana at will seeking trout for sport, and solitude for prayer and thinking. I spent my years in Montana as a full-time wanderer. I wandered through books, my parish, and through fields and streams. No matter what I was doing on the outside, I was wandering in prayer and thought on the inside. I didn't fish every day, but I fished a lot more than I wanted to admit. I think the people knew. They didn't seem to care. The churches did quite well. Whatever it was I was doing—I least of all knew what I was doing—it seemed to be working.

The entire ministry flowed from the long wandering thinking in the presence of God. My preaching, calling and leadership arose from fishing and praying. The churches grew, they became financially sound for the first time in their histories, and they developed a stable foundation of lay leadership for ongoing ministry. How a stable foundation for ministry springs from walking around aimlessly and praying whatever comes to mind is beyond me, but apparently it is not beyond the reality of long wandering prayer. Ministry is all grace. If my work had flowed from days praying on my knees, perhaps I could connect the dots of discipline, compliance and method to prayer and ministry. Perhaps then I could connect my ministry with my efforts. But going out and fishing while thinking about the problems in the church is not work to be proud of. It's embarrassing.

Now I live in Cincinnati, Ohio. Replacing my popgun, skateboard and fly rod are my golf clubs. When I golf alone, I can pray just like when I fished. The way I golf, I still wander a great deal. I can't golf in Ohio as much as I fished in Montana, but the Cincinnati area has many parks and trails with huge, old deciduous trees and many streams—perfect for walking and praying.

Do Other People Pray This Way?

I am willing to concede that my prayer habit may be eccentric. As I have already said, this form of prayer is an adaptation of my normal way of thinking. I walked for hours to think before I walked for hours to pray. So will people who have not walked to think be able to walk to pray? Maybe not. Nevertheless, I know that many Christians walk to think. Can they learn to walk to pray? I'm sure they can. I know positively that many Christians have prayed long wandering prayers during times of crisis. Why can't they learn to do it regularly? I feel certain that many Christians would like to pray long wandering prayers. They talk about wanting to spend a day with God, but they report failing and quitting. I believe they fail because they have tried praying all day with disciplined methods that work spectacularly for some but lead most of us to failure.

My morning devotions are a matter of discipline. My long prayers are a matter of appetite. I don't pray all day unless I want to. I go out and pray long when I am thirsty for God. I pray all day when I need to exchange my anxious thoughts for the peace that passes understanding, when I want to know the truth that sets free, when I am out on a limb and the branch is cracking, when I feel lonely and I want the presence of the Beloved. The Spirit creates the desire in my soul, and I follow my will. God's open ear is irresistible to me because he has given me a new heart. God's Spirit speaks to my new heart, compelling me to pray lengthy, bitter prayers of repentance for the old Adam still at work within me. One day of prayer sounds like a psalm of praise, another sounds like Romans 7. Most days sound like a little of both.

Maybe it's a confession of weakness, but I can't pray for more than an hour unless I'm doing something else, whether it's listening to birds in a wood or hacking at a golf ball. Most Christians who think of going out and praying all day want to do something more weighty sounding than praying and golfing. But sometimes what's happening on the outside is very different from what's happening on the inside. A hike in a beautiful wilderness on the outside may conceal clawing-by-fingernails progress through a wasteland on the inside. If the activity on the outside is trivial (fishing), but the activity on the inside is life changing (repentance), why feel guilty about calling it prayer? Because people don't understand? If I can pray all day while I fish or golf or bird watch due to my weakness, isn't that better than spending the day not praying because I can't address God in a grand, disciplined way? Isn't it better to pray the way we can, instead of not praying because we can't pray the way we think other people pray?

Still, I waited to write a book about long wandering prayer until I had at least a little evidence that I could set a person free to pray. The opportunity to test this occurred in 1996 when David Horn, director of the Shoemaker Center for Church Renewal at Gordon-Conwell Theological Seminary, contacted me and asked if I would come to Gordon-Conwell to give a one-day seminar for pastors. I talked with him about teaching on long wandering prayer, and he decided I should try it.

The ideas intrigued most of the pastors. More than I expected had already prayed long wandering prayers and were encouraged to hear someone claim it and name it. Others expressed thanks for the freedom. They had never been told that wandering around aimlessly talking to themselves in the presence of God was one of the pastor's main responsibilities. Two years after the seminar I was in Maine speaking to pastors. A pastor at the conference told me that he had attended the seminar at Gordon-Conwell. He told me that the talks on prayer had convinced him to find a place on the coast near his home where he could pray alone. He reported that the practice had transformed his ministry.

Another encouraging response came from an unexpected source. The receptionist for the Shoemaker Center had listened to the seminar. Six months after the seminar she called me on the phone to tell me that she had prayed long wandering-type prayers for years and that my talks had encouraged her to resume the practice regularly.

That was the spark I needed to write the book. Furthermore, her call convinced me that I needed prayer narratives of Christians already praying long wandering prayers. I asked her if I wrote a book on this subject, if she would be willing to try writing a prayer narrative for the book. She agreed that she would try. The results of her first attempts were so wonderful that I felt quite sure that I could find more people to do the same thing. Finding people willing to write about their long wandering prayers was not difficult. I have scattered these prayer narratives throughout the book. The voices of the prayer narratives are different from mine, and they are different from each other. It may jangle you a little to read different voices. However I believe these testimonies of prayer will deepen your understanding of long wandering prayer. Another writer's experiences may allow you to see yourself praying.

Is There Any Reasonable Biblical Model for This Kind of Prayer?

So, some people go out and wander around talking to God. Are there any reasonable biblical models for this kind of prayer? The apostle Paul tells us to "pray without ceasing" (1 Thess 5:17). What can he mean by that? Can it really mean talk to God in the second person singular all day long? Perhaps he means for us to open all of our thinking to God as a form of prayer. The psalmists appear to pray this way.

The Psalms are the prayer book and the hymnbook of the Bible. God's people have been praying them and singing them for thousands of years. The Psalms were the hymnal of the synagogue in Jesus' day. If you have prayed through the Psalms, or if you have turned to them in times of need, you may have noticed some peculiarities there that stretch our definition of prayer. The most famous psalm of all, Psalm 23, the Shepherd Psalm, starts with David talking to himself. "The LORD is my shepherd, I shall not want." He doesn't address God in the second person singular until he says, "Even though I walk through the darkest valley, I fear no evil; for you are with me." The whole psalm is prayer. But how can it be prayer if David shifts back and forth between talking to himself and talking to God?

In Psalm 42, the unnamed psalmist begins in the second person singular:

As a deer longs for flowing streams,
    so my soul longs for you, O God. (Ps 42:1)

The prayer shifts immediately to the first person singular:

My soul thirsts for God, for the living God.

When shall I come and behold the face of God? (Ps 42:2)

Obviously psalm praying is much more than just talking to God in the second person singular. Psalm praying appears to be a running inner dialogue in the presence of God. Many of the psalms appear to be poetic compressions of hours alone wrestling with God and self and even with enemies and loved ones. In some cases the psalmist appears to be talking to an enemy or a loved one not present at the time of the prayer. Can it be prayer to talk to people who aren't even there?

In Psalm 55, David begins praying directly to God. He is in pain:

Give ear to my prayer, O God;
   do not hide yourself from my supplication.
Attend to me, and answer me;
   I am troubled in my complaint. (Ps 55:1-2)

He is in pain over an enemy:

I am distraught by the noise of the enemy,
   because of the clamor of the wicked.
For they bring trouble upon me,
   and in anger they cherish enmity against me. (Ps 55:2-3)

His pain is unto death. He is experiencing terrors, trembling and dread:

My heart is in anguish within me,
   the terrors of death have fallen upon me.
Fear and trembling come upon me,
   and horror overwhelms me. (Ps 55:4-5)

He confesses to God what he has told himself in this crisis. He wants nothing more than to flee:

And I say, "O that I had wings like a dove!
   I would fly away and be at rest;

truly, I would flee far away;
   I would lodge in the wilderness;
               Selah
I would hurry to find a shelter for myself
   from the raging wind and tempest." (Ps 55:6-8)

David calls upon the Lord to discredit his enemies, for they are wreaking havoc in the city of God:

Confuse, O Lord, confound their speech;
   for I see violence and strife in the city.
Day and night they go around it on its walls,
and iniquity and trouble are within it;
   ruin is in its midst;
oppression and fraud do not depart from its marketplace.
      (Ps 55:9-11)

Now the mood shifts from desperation and anger to melancholy. He's talking to himself—or is he talking to someone else? He is either recalling a conversation with a friend who has turned on him, or he is carrying on a mock conversation with this former friend, in his mind, in the presence of God—as a form of prayer:

It is not enemies who taunt me—
   I could bear that;
it is not adversaries who deal insolently with me—
   I could hide from them.
But it is you, my equal, my companion, my familiar friend,
with whom I kept pleasant company;
   we walked in the house of God with the throng. (Ps 55:12-14)

David utters a curse upon his turncoat brother and his consorts:

Let death come upon them;
   let them go down alive to Sheol;
     for evil is in their homes and in their hearts. (Ps 55:15)

How can he do this? Is this truly God's will for our prayers? Are we supposed to call down fire from heaven on those who hurt us? Or is David letting his mind go in the presence of God? He curses his enemies because that is what his heart feels. His heart, mind and soul are totally open to God. We have a difficult time imagining prayer this honest.

But David's mood shifts again. He doesn't dwell on the curse. He decides to mind his own business and let God be the judge. For his part, he will call upon the Lord and trust in the Lord. Who is being addressed here?

> But I call upon God,
>   and the LORD will save me.
> Evening and morning and at noon
>   I utter my complaint and moan,
>   and he will hear my voice.
> He will redeem me unharmed
>   from the battle that I wage,
>   for many are arrayed against me.
> God, who is enthroned from of old,
>
> *Selah*
>
> will hear, and will humble them—
> because they do not change, and do not fear God. (Ps 55:16-19)

We hear the reason for the hurt. David's former friend broke a promise and secretly schemed against him. Who is he talking to here?

> My companion laid hands on a friend
>   and violated a covenant with me
> with speech smoother than butter,
>   but with a heart set on war;
> with words that were softer than oil,
>   but in fact were drawn swords. (Ps 55:20-21)

He teaches the congregation. Is he talking to the congregation in person, or is he talking to the congregation in an inner dialogue, the same way he spoke to his former friend?

> Cast your burden on the LORD,
>   and he will sustain you;
> he will never permit the righteous to be moved. (Ps 55:22)

It sounds like he must be talking to the congregation in his mind. He shifts back to addressing God in the second person:

> But you, O God, will cast them down
>   into the lowest pit;
> the bloodthirsty and treacherous
>   shall not live out half their days.
> But I will trust in you. (Ps 55:23)

Psalm 55 is a prayer that is a story of a prayer. It recounts in short what David prayed at length. It is a poetic compression of a long and arduous prayer. This explains the dramatic shifts in address and in personal mood in such a short space. For instance, praying in utter honesty, David calls a curse on his enemy. It doesn't last long. It doesn't exactly say that he repented of this outburst, but his mood swings to the confession that he will instead trust God to protect him and to vindicate him. Putting this in New Testament terms, David changed from the feelings of the disciples James and John, who asked Jesus: "Lord, do you want us to command fire to come down from heaven and consume them?" (Lk 9:54-55) to the good sense of the apostle Paul who said, "Beloved, never avenge yourselves, but leave room for the wrath of God; for it is written, 'Vengeance is mine, I will repay, says the Lord'" (Rom 12:19).

Have you wondered how a psalmist can move emotionally from being distraught over God's apparent disappearance to expressing love and hope and praise in a prayer that takes one minute to pray? In Psalm 13 David begins with a cry of anguish:

> How long, O LORD? Will you forget me forever?

How long will you hide your face from me? (Ps 13:1)

A few sentences later he confesses his absolute trust and praise:

But I trusted in your steadfast love;
    my heart shall rejoice in your salvation.
I will sing to the LORD,
    because he has dealt bountifully with me. (Ps 13:5-6)

We want to end prayer praising God, but it usually takes us longer then this. How long should it take? How long did it take David to come to his senses? Thirty seconds? This psalm is a poetic compression of a much longer prayer. The poem recounts in a minute a spiritual reformation that took hours or even days of personal anguish.

How else can we explain how certain psalms change topics so quickly and unpredictably in the middle of prayer? If some of the psalms compress long experiences, then the shifts in voice, subject and emotion reflect the shifts of the longer prayer. Perhaps psalm praying means praying the psalms in short and praying long prayers like the prayers at the root of the psalms. Go out and open your mind before God in a long wandering process of psalm-like praying.

Praying the psalms changed the aim and order for my prayers. Some of the grisliest psalms end in hope and praise. Often I can not wrestle through a problem to honest hope and praise in two minutes. I can however hold on to hope and praise as the goal of every prayer, no matter how long it takes and no matter how many emotional and cognitive shifts it takes to get there. This instruction in prayer comes to me from the psalms, but it corresponds to the desire in my heart. That it takes me so long to pray to hope and praise is, well, reality. If it takes me a day to move through sin and despair to hope and praise, that's the way it is. But the journey to hope and praise is worth any amount of time and any amount of mental effort. That's why long wandering prayer is not a matter of discipline, it is a matter of desire. It isn't about compliance to law; it's about hunger for grace. Hunger for grace comes from God's grace. Thus long wandering prayer never feels like an accomplishment. This makes it difficult to talk about because saying how it happens is hard.

Order of the Subject

My book on long wandering prayer roams a bit. After all, a book on disjointed thought sequences requires a discursive narrative. (I take solace in the fact that *discursive* is defined as both *"Passing rapidly or irregularly from one subject to another; rambling, digressive; extending over or dealing with a wide range of subjects,"* and *"Passing from premises to conclusions; proceeding by reasoning or argument; ratiocinative."*)[1] I do hope that both can be true! Nevertheless I really did try to write in a logical order.

Chapter One. "Long Prayer" is about the potential for long prayer and some of the barriers. A recently retired woman who lived most of her life in Maryland writes the personal prayer narrative.

Chapter Two. "Wandering Prayer" is about the role of physical and mental wandering in prayer. I hope to show why physical motion during prayer extends the life of prayer and enriches its content. The personal prayer narrative is by a young pastor who hikes the Rockies, walks the campus of the University of Wyoming and gets worked up at his son's Little League baseball games.

Chapter Three. "Long Wandering Vision" is about what we see on the inside in long wandering prayer. Often we see pictures of previously uncorrelated events connecting for the first time. Often these mental pictures become visions. The prayer narrative is by me.

Chapter Four. "Battering the Heart of God" is about bringing our petitions to God repeatedly with little respect for courtesy. They used to call it "importunity." If boxing God with our prayers is the requirement, then long wandering prayer is like going all twelve rounds. I write the prayer narrative.

Chapter Five. "Worthless Guilt About Things That Don't Apply" is about our guilt-ridden excuses that often keep us from long prayer. As the narrative, a women living in New England recounts how guilty she felt taking time away from her young family to spend time with God.

Chapter Six. "How Can Something I'm So Bad At Be God's Will for My Life?" is about the fact that very often a day of long prayer is dry as dirt. Is this because we're bad at prayer? Maybe—except—some prayers we feel worst about are really our best prayers. Many hours of spiritual emptiness make us ask the deep questions we avoid in shorter prayers. The prayer narrative is by an American pastor presently teaching in a seminary in Lithuania. This is a hard chapter.

Chapter Seven. "The Good Stuff" is about the outrageous, wonderful experiences with God and answered prayer in long wandering prayer. How can we describe them? How can we keep powerful experiences in prayer from ruining prayer? The personal prayer narrative is by a young mother who lived on Cape Cod and now lives in Atlanta.

One

Long Prayer

All Christians aspire to long prayer. Some feel it acutely, others barely at all. As sons and daughters of Adam and Eve there is latent in each of us the desire to walk with God in the cool of the evening. As children of Jacob we are required at critical points in our lives to wrestle all night with the angel of the Lord. As those whose spiritual parents trekked with Jesus around Judea, there exists in us the desire to do the same. (I dare say that if the prospect of spending a day wandering the shore of the Sea of Galilee with Jesus of Nazareth is abhorrent to you, you may not be a Christian.) Finally, we need not be children of Enoch to be impressed by the outcome of his life of long prayer: "Enoch walked with God; then he was no more, because God took him" (Gen 5:24).

Who among us does not long for the personal experience of the apostle Paul's gracious command: "Do not worry about anything, but in everything by prayer and supplication with thanksgiving let your requests be made known to God. And the peace of God, which surpasses all understanding, will guard your hearts and your minds in Christ Jesus" (Phil 4:6-7). We would gladly unload our anxiety on God and walk away at peace, if we only knew how. It says "pray." Many Christians have tried releasing their worries to God in prayer, but frankly it just hasn't worked. That is, short prayers haven't worked. How can short prayer solve the problem of long worry? It took a long time for anxiety to grip our guts; only long prayer can release that power.

We ache for social justice, and we believe that prayer changes the world. What kind of prayer changes the world? The prophet Amos says, "Take away from me the noise of your songs; I will not listen to the melody of your harps. But let justice roll down like waters, and righteousness like an ever-flowing stream" (Amos 5:23-24). Religion that cranks adrenaline but creates no space for peace in life and society is trivial. We sense the need to roll up our sleeves and get to work. But we don't know where or how. The issues become more complex, not less. We feel the need to "strike while the iron is hot," but we don't know where to apply the blow. We need God's help to unravel layers of injustice that go back many generations. Can a one-minute prayer solve a hundred-year problem? Maybe, but not likely.

In his Gospel, Mark tells us that "In the morning, while it was still very dark, [Jesus] got up and went out to a deserted place, and there he prayed" (Mk 1:35). Jesus taught, healed and exorcised demons hour upon hour every day. Whenever he could, he slipped away to a solitary place to pray. He prayed short, and he prayed long. Could he have just prayed short? Would a prayer here and there have kept his compassion furnace stoked for the two-hundredth encounter on a normal day? Could momentary supplications have kept him on the road to the cross? If Jesus needed to leave and pray long to keep his ministry on track and powered up, is it possible that we require less? But what does it mean to leave home and go off to a solitary place to pray? He did it. Can we do it?

We Feel Frustrated

Most of us feel deeply frustrated. We have tried long prayer and have come up short. Our mind cannot scratch our soul's itch. It seems a sure bet that more discipline is the solution. But when discipline seems like the solution, our problem-solving skills have thrown the fight for dirty money. The Accuser bets his stake on the power of guilt to discourage us. Guilt crushes our imagination's power to show us new ways. Our aspirations heave, gasp, wheeze and go comatose.

We deal with our stymied yearning to be with God differently. For some, long prayer is a dream set in another life in which the demands of existence cannot interrupt the divine-human encounter. For others, long prayer is a desire shoved unconscious, a nightmare of unkept promises and hasty boasts. For others, the idea of long prayer is emblematic of the disappointment that nurses their doubt. A small but significant set possesses an aching thirst for God unquenchable by anything but complete possession by the divine host (Enoch types). Still others pray long when there is trouble (Jacob types), but when the crisis is past, the urge subsides.

I have belonged to these groups during my thirty years as a Christian. But I have spent most of my twenty years as a pastor in the crisis-management prayer group. The daily exigencies of my life have not precluded prayer; they have demanded it. My guilt over past failures at prayer never hurt as much as the crises requiring prayer. I have ignored prayer only to be reawakened by soul-wrenching circumstances. My burning desire to be with God has normally been the prayer desire: "O that I had wings like a dove! I would fly away and be at rest" (Ps 55:6).

For me, the high aspiration of spending long, unhurried time with God has nearly always been instigated by a simple cry for help. I leave my office to find a place where I can wander alone and pray long, to plead for an answer to a problem. Along the way my desire to be with God is satisfied whether or not prayer settles the initial irritant.

In fact, irritance may be the number one reason why Christians go out and pray for a long time. So be it. For myself, my best motives for prayer and my worst motives for prayer are never far apart. They are like positive one and negative one on a number line. The midpoint they share is zero. This book is not about "correct motives for prayer." We don't need better motives for prayer; we need better power for prayer. On that count, we don't need fuel; we need freedom. As P. T. Forsyth (1848-1921) observed: "We are never so active and so free as in prayer to an absolutely free God."[1]

This book is an invitation to enter the school of hard knocks of long prayer. Be forewarned that you will experience failure on almost every step of this pilgrim road. If you cannot bear to fail, you cannot bear long prayer. If you must measure success, you won't need a long tape. (How can you measure the invisible soul communing with the omnipresent Spirit?) Human success at long prayer cannot be weighed, counted or marked. If you got good grades in school, long prayer may be difficult for you. Long prayer is simply not a human achievement.

Praying Out of Doors
Long wandering prayer is not normally indoor prayer. Elijah didn't hear the still small voice in a library. Jesus suggests that some kinds of prayer require the observation of nature firsthand.

> Therefore I tell you, do not worry about your life, what you will eat, or about your body, what you will wear. For life is more than food, and the body more than clothing. Consider the ravens: they neither sow nor reap, they have neither storehouse nor barn, and yet God feeds them. Of how much more value are you than the birds! And can any of you by worrying add a single hour to your span of life? If then you are not able to do so small a thing as that, why do you

worry about the rest? Consider the lilies, how they grow: they neither toil nor spin; yet I tell you, even Solomon in all his glory was not clothed like one of these. But if God so clothes the grass of the field, which is alive today and tomorrow is thrown into the oven, how much more will he clothe you—you of little faith! And do not keep striving for what you are to eat and what you are to drink, and do not keep worrying. For it is the nations of the world that strive after all these things, and your Father knows that you need them. Instead, strive for his kingdom, and these things will be given to you as well. (Lk 12:22-31)

In this well-known and deeply admired passage Jesus portrays his vision of true happiness. It is a life of service in the kingdom of God in which the same Lord who clothes and feeds flowers and birds cares for us, freeing us from the crippling anxiety that destroys our lives. As wonderful as this picture is, many of us find it difficult to believe that this could become our operative vision for life. Another way to put it is that we cannot imagine not worrying. We know that worry hurts us and those around us. We drop worry off at a prayer meeting, but it stalks us home.

We know that worry dissipates our usefulness to the kingdom. We know that we would give more money to kingdom work if we weren't so worried about having enough money to face our uncertain future. We know that we waste a lot of mental energy in worry —it saps our strength to study the Word and seek fellowship. Worry leaves us with just enough energy to sit in front of the TV and watch newsmagazine shows that show us ever-new threats to our lives.

Some Christians ban worry rather easily (we sense it may be some kind of genetic advantage). For the rest of us, relax. Jesus does not teach that we can rid ourselves of worry with a wink. He teaches something far simpler and quite practical: *consider the ravens . . . consider the lilies . . . and the grass of the field.* What can it mean to *consider the ravens*? On the one hand it must mean more than just *watch the ravens,* and on the other hand it must mean more than just *think abstractly about the ravens.* Speaking personally, my imagination is vivid and my thinking is abstract, but just thinking about ravens doesn't help me. I need to go out and watch birds and think about what birds do and let God minister to me through what I see them doing. To get the full effect I must *consider the ravens*—in person.

Jesus spoke to an agrarian society, and he presupposed that his audience sees ravens, lilies and fields of grass nearly every day. However, he does not presuppose that his listeners will take time to think about ravens, lilies and God. Many rural people today don't think much about the natural world around them and presumably many rural people back then did not do so either. How about city folks? At the time the four Gospels were written, Christian faith was largely an urban phenomenon. It is highly significant that Luke and Matthew felt that their urban brothers and sisters—Christians whose daily encounter with nature amounted to donkey plop in streets—needed to consider ravens, lilies and fields, and presumably in person.

You live in a city. Does it have to be a raven? Why not a pigeon? Or a sea gull? Pigeons and sea gulls are urban ravens. Do your city parks have flowers? Lawns? Trees? Is it impossible for you to travel to the country for a walk? Most nursing home residents can sit in a courtyard where their chances of seeing a sparrow are quite good.

Should you bring a Bible or binoculars? Is this bird watching or is it prayer? Could it be both? Jesus implies that for this kind of prayer binoculars will be sufficient.

Suppose you are walking in a forest, talking with God, and you hear the *tap, tap, tap* of a woodpecker. You break off the trail and off your talk to God to look for the woodpecker—have you stopped praying? Not if by seeking the woodpecker you are "considering the ravens." If Jesus asks us to *consider the ravens* as a way of striving for the kingdom, isn't straining to see a woodpecker a kind of striving after the kingdom? Are there no birds in the kingdom?

If you sight the bird, identify it, watch it smash its beak into a tree for twenty minutes and come away more joyful. If your talk with God takes on a decidedly thankful turn, then I suggest that seeking the woodpecker and watching it closely was prayer.

The beauty of creation reflects the glory of God. It is more than spiritual. If Jesus wanted us to think of spiritual beauty, he might have asked us to consider a beautiful idea or a beautiful law or even a beautiful story. But Jesus asks us to consider the lilies—members of God's creation that cannot think, tell stories or do good deeds. They're pretty and smell good, and that's it. When Jesus wants us to calm our worries, he doesn't tell us to think about spiritual beauty. He bids us to consider the lilies.

We all want to look good. I take communion to a shut-in woman who is 110 years old. She is blind, cannot walk, weighs around eighty pounds and is nearly deaf in one ear. On a recent visit I asked her if she knew how old she was. She said, "I think I'm more than 100 years old." "Yes, you are more than 100 years old. In fact, you are 110 years old." "Oh! That is very old," she replied. "Yes, and for your 110th birthday your picture was in the paper." "Was it a good picture?" she asked. "Yes, it was a very nice picture." "That's good," she said. It is not vain to want to be beautiful because it is not prideful for God to reveal his glory.

Jesus wants us to be lily watchers not clothes hogs. Lilies don't complain to God about wearing the same color every day. Canyons don't complain to God that their rock formations change only every ten thousand years. And yet on my fiftieth walk up a particular canyon I see new things, just because the light is different than before. It isn't the clothing. It's the light.

So how is this prayer? Well, if you take your lunch to a botanical garden near where you work and walk along looking at the plants, and you thank God for the beauty of creation and for the grace he gives some people to collect and display plants, that is prayer. And I suspect that you will walk away feeling far less anxious about your life than if you had spent that hour in your office or even in a church, trying to pray the whole time, feeling anxious and guilty that your mind wandered.

Much of our anxiety comes from our loathing of death. In a discourse on inner peace we might not expect Jesus to ask us to meditate on dead stuff, but he does: "But if God so clothes the grass of the field, which is alive today and tomorrow is thrown into the oven . . ." (Lk 12:28). That's a nice thought—meditate on the fact that all the pretty grass will burn. How can that help?

On a hike in a forest, climbing over downed trees, sinking a foot into a peat bog, considering shriveled up lilies, it occurs to us that stuff dies and so do we. Death comes from the Fall of humanity and is our enemy, but much worse things can happen to us than dying—like going to hell for instance. Our Savior tells us, "Do not fear those who kill the body but cannot kill the soul; rather fear him who can destroy both soul and body in hell" (Mt 10:28). Watching fields grow and die teaches us that we can grow, though we will die. If fearing death precludes loving life, our fear of death may be worse than death; in fact, the fear of death may be the real enemy in death.

We go out to pray long for friends who are sick. We have a list. We pray for the people on the list but maybe not in the order we planned. Along the way our eyes may fix upon a symbol of death, a field of grass burning or an abandoned building, and without warning we feel sad or angry. If we allow our minds to wander through these thoughts in the presence of God with plenty of time, we will find that we are indeed quite concerned about our own mortality. We must bear this concern before the Lord along with our concern for our sick friends. When our prayers shift from what we wanted to talk about—our sick friends—to what we did not want to talk about—our dread of our own mortality—and then shift back to our sick friends, we pray with real hope because our prayers are born of compassion instead of our fear of death. But we went out to pray for our friends. Isn't it self-centered to pray about our own mortality? When our mind wandered from focusing on others to focusing upon ourselves, isn't that the definition of self-centeredness? Unless our mind wanders in the presence of God, we can never discover that really we went out to pray for ourselves as well as for our loved ones. We are praying for their healing, and we are praying for our grief and for our fear all at the same time. It needs to be that way. We cannot pray well for our loved ones unless we are also willing to pray well for ourselves. We aren't good at begging God to save the life of our loved ones until we have come to terms with our own death. Until we come to terms with our own death, we aren't just praying for our loved ones. We are praying for ourselves; we're praying for our own grief, our own anger, our own loss, our own fear. You can't pray for someone else to be healed until you yourself are unafraid to die. Your mind can only wander into this insight. You can never discover this praying down a list. You can only pray this way when God takes your mind from what you wanted to pray about to what really needs to be prayed about. Very often, when God takes our mind away from what we wanted to pray about to what we really need to pray about, it feels like our mind has wandered. If you quit praying when your mind begins to wander, perhaps you are quitting before you have even begun to know God in prayer.

I insist that long wandering prayer is not giving up control of your mind, rather it is not insisting upon tightening the screws on your mind, to insist on thinking about one thing when we pray. It isn't letting anything happen, but it is a refusal to control precisely what happens—as lovers talk as they wander.

Long wandering prayer is not like a meeting with your boss or your ruling board. It is like lovers wandering with one another, without a plan, without hiding thoughts, not knowing where the trip will lead—and not caring. Yes, such moments are risky. Disagreements surface and wrangling ensues, but not without a purpose and rarely without time to settle grievances. And because the Other is the Beloved, the desire to wander and speak will be renewed again and again. The following experience from one Montana woman illustrates how prayer reconnects us to God.

A Prayer Narrative

For eighteen years every Monday I hiked along the rivers and reservoirs, creeks and streams and in the hardwood forests of Maryland. Not knowing at the beginning what would evolve out of making this commitment, what riches of Spirit and Presence, I agreed to it. My husband and I had been hiking with our three young children for several years on our vacations each summer in the Rocky Mountains of northwestern Montana. I enjoyed it. I knew that our children were benefiting from watching my husband and me observing and learning ourselves as we identified the trees, the exquisite and abundant wildflowers with their similarities, their differences, their adaptations to crevices in rock facings along cascading mountain streams (that would never work if *I* tried planting them there). We learned the names of the creatures—the pika, the hoary marmot, which changes his coat color to white in the wintertime, the grizzly bear with his silver-tipped hump over his neck, the mountain goats with their foot pads that enable them to balance on high, rocky cliffs, the bighorn sheep, the weasel weaseling in and out of rock fissures. We studied the formations of rock and how they came to be—the Lewis Overthrust, the tectonic plates, glacial moraines, cirques,

U-shaped glacial valleys, aretes, hanging valleys. And we observed the bird life—the pileated and Lewis's woodpeckers, the raucous Steller's jays and Clark's nutcrackers, the huge golden and bald eagles. And observing and unconsciously taking note of patterns, habits and traits at some point helped me realize deep within me how congruent the natural world is with my soul, unlike the world of technology that seems so grating and unnatural—incongruent—with that still, small voice of God within me.

So when my husband suggested that the two of us start hiking on Mondays (our "day off" from parish work), it was familiar and so enjoyable from doing it in the summers that I was game to try it year round. Maryland, fall through spring; Montana, part of the summers.

We bought all kinds of weather gear so we could go out regardless of the conditions because we knew we wouldn't go much of the time if left to week-by-week decision making. I don't think there were very many Mondays when I felt like going. I had just sent three children out the door to school with their home-packed lunches. Sunday had been demanding for me, as well as my pastor-husband, and I was tired. But the decision was in place, no question—go. And we did. Harder yet, for the extroverted, gregarious person that I am, after a year or so of our Monday hiking routine, my husband suggested that we enter into silence at the trailhead and not come out of the silence until lunchtime. So each Monday after we parked at the trailhead, I read a psalm, prayed for us, and we then kept the silence. By the time we stopped for lunch at noon after finding a flat rock on the river or a log on the trail to sit on, nearly all we talked about was what we had observed on the trail, maybe some of our impressions of what we saw, perhaps how hard it had been to shed the things going on inside us. As we turned

around to hike back to our car, it was strange to me that all I
wanted to do by then was be quiet, observe and just *be*. I remember saying to my husband on the way home one day, "You know,
I really didn't feel like going this morning, but God never disap-
points me. It seems like he always meets me here. I always
leave the trail feeling more whole, more put together. And I
know it sounds a little strange, but today several times I just felt
like hugging God."

I didn't start out feeling this way. It began with feeling happy
just to be with my husband. Pastoring can be very demanding
much of the time, with little emotional energy left over for the
dearest one in your life. So for much of one day each week—
Monday on our hikes—I could have him all to myself. But I began to feel something else was going on too.

After hiking for about nine months' worth of Mondays, we
went to the Pocono Mountains of Pennsylvania on a retreat with
Douglas Steere, a Quaker. We didn't know it ahead of time, but
when we got to the retreat center he called us into a silent retreat with talks by him interspersed through the weekend. One
of the talks was about walking to Emmaus, recounting the story
of the two disciples fleeing Jerusalem after the crucifixion, not
knowing Christ had risen and was alive, and being met on the
road, conversing, eating together with a fellow traveler, later realizing when they broke bread with the stranger and he disappeared that the one had been Jesus.

Steere met with each of the people on the retreat individually
during the weekend so we could have a personal conversation
together. My husband and I went together for our appointed
time, and as we shared with Steere about our Monday walks,
"our eyes were opened" at the realization that we had been
meeting Jesus on these walks and now recognized why they had
become so meaningful to us. It felt a little electrifying to me to

have that named for what it was. And our Monday hikes entered a new dimension for me.

Because these long wandering prayers meant so much to me, I started offering a day of silence in a wooded area of our church camp/conference center to a group of women who were meeting regularly for Bible study and intercessory prayer through the year. It became a highlight of the year together when each spring at the end of our study, we would travel a few miles north to the woods of southeastern Pennsylvania to enjoy in community a day of silent walking and praying. How blessed those days were for me, to wander in silence in community, to see others obviously enjoying the silence and the prayer wandering. I saw Barbara wandering and praying, knowing a little about her unhappy marriage and feeling such a kinship with her in her struggles to stay with the marriage and make it work, maybe even make it into a good marriage one day. And I saw Cynthia, who was the caregiver for her husband with Parkinson's disease, and all the pain in her own life of how to help him live these days out in joy and goodness together. The same nucleus of women continues to host these silent retreats each spring even though I have moved away and new leadership has taken over.

We also introduced a time of prayer wandering on our youth confirmation retreats each spring as my husband and I gave them time to walk and pray and think about their commitment to Jesus Christ as they prepared to join the church. It sounds risky to attempt this with noisy, active, fidgety young people, but they were some of the most appreciative of the quietness: Kim, who so enjoyed athletics but had to modify her ambitions because of monitoring Chrohns disease; Joe, whose mother had earlier committed suicide, now having to learn how to adjust to a new stepmother and siblings. By being able to join them in their confusions, struggles and tough knocks of life in this silent prayer time, we somehow knew deep within that this makes a difference. (We spent time with them preparing them for the time alone and "decompression" time afterward talking about their experience.)

We live in such a noisy, distracting world. The soul tends to get neglected first. Many people, I think, are not even aware of this center, this core within them we call *soul*. I have found it rewarding to introduce and give opportunity to people to meet that center within themselves.

When I experience the silence, I find I can be comfortable with myself after a while and allow myself to get acquainted with the real me instead of the person wearing a mask with others, as well as with myself. Because I have been doing this kind of long wandering prayer for so many years, I find my soul thirsts for it if I go too long without it, almost like how the body that is used to regular physical exercise cries out for it if neglected. The body and mind crave it. So it is with exercising the soul muscles.

Initially I didn't know the long-term benefits of taking these prayer walks, but now I do. Lest this sound all that "spiritual" an exercise, often I just *see* in a new way the light playing on a tree trunk, the colorful lichen on a boulder helping to break it down into soil over the years, inviting the natural world to help me empty myself so that God can fill me with his presence, his agenda for me. Often these are times when I feel so loved by him.

I've probably never had a major revelation or been spoken to by God with my ears as some claim, but my walk with God has been deepened and enriched by these Emmaus walks where I have recognized him and experienced this joyful desire to hug him. And because I cannot hug him physically, I think my response must go deeper within and hopefully make a long-term difference in the way I live out my Christian walk.

In Faith We Seek the Beloved

Long wandering prayer is our practical striving, in faith, to know the Beloved through the darkness, trouble and sin of life. Jesus told us, "In the world ye shall have tribulation: but be of good cheer; I have overcome the world" (Jn 16:33 KJV). In faith we believe that Jesus has truly overcome the world; in prayer we seek to know, through the gloom, the face we so long to see. Long prayer is faith's practical vehicle for our long journey to penetrate much darkness. Long prayer is thinking through what is known to what is not known in the presence of the willing object of our investigation— the living God.

Teachers of Christian faith down through the centuries testify that faith is certainty in the face of inescapable ambiguity. Faith is an act of love in which we reach to the Beloved through the dark. In faith we embrace God, not ambiguity. Darkness is no barrier to faith because faith is a gift of the Beloved we embrace! So faith reaches to embrace our Beloved through ambiguity, bidden by the Beloved, with doubt about our ability to reach the Lord—thus faith—but without doubt about the veracity of the One who calls to us. So faith is a peculiar kind of knowing, but it is the best kind of knowing. And in the end, our most certain kind of knowing. Faith does not take us beyond human knowing so much as it takes the frailty of our perception and cognition with absolute seriousness.

Faith wills to know the Beloved. Faith desires to comprehend the Beloved, not to conquer but to rejoice in mutual understanding. We rejoice to know God in trinitarian splendor, and we rejoice to know that we are dust, for it is God's perfect will for us. As dust we barely know ourselves, but in faith we know that we are known and loved by God, and this is quite enough. To know ourselves correctly means to will to know ourselves as we are known by the Beloved. The ambiguity through which we reach to the Beloved derives precisely from our ingrained, rebel will to know ourselves as ourselves, apart from the One who loves us. We despise our will to know ourselves apart from the Beloved who loves us, but this does not mean that we necessarily despise the ambiguity through which we reach to the Beloved. We do not embrace the darkness! Neither, however, need we fear it. Mysteriously, painful ambiguity catalyzes our "sweet hour of prayer."

Our path is not dark to him. We are known and loved. We desire with all our heart to know and love in return, for this is the unquenchable desire of all love, to know and be known. So faith cannot desire to understand the Beloved less, it can only desire to know more and more fully the meaning that God is love. This means that ultimately faith must hope to see the Beloved face to face. With the early Christians we pray, "Come quickly, Lord Jesus!" But for now we live for the moments in which we glimpse, if only fleetingly, the glory of God. Jonathan Edwards writes,

> Once, as I rode out into the woods for my health, in 1737, having alighted from my horse in a retired place, as my manner commonly has been to walk for divine contemplation and prayer, I had a view, that for me was extraordinary, of the glory of the Son of God, as Mediator between God and man, and his wonderful, great, full, pure and sweet grace and love, and meek and gentle condescension.[2]

T w o

Wandering Prayer

Prayer comes to us from a people who spent the first thousand years of their existence living in tents. From Abraham to David, the Hebrews were a shepherding, moving folk. They lived out-of-doors easily, though not painlessly. Following the scent of green pastures, they passed through death valleys, ascended passes and crossed rivers. Wandering lay at the core of their psyche from the beginning, and it shaped their life with God.

The night sky fills their prayers. They praised God for heavy dew. They pleaded for deliverance from flash floods. Drought meant death. This caused their more settled cousin peoples, the Canaanites, to worship gods of storm and cloud. But during drought the Hebrews could move, and so they did. They never traveled to a place where Yahweh did not demonstrate his lordship.

> Where can I go from your spirit?
> Or where can I flee from your presence?
> If I ascend to heaven, you are there;
> if I make my bed in Sheol, you are there.
> If I take the wings of the morning

and settle at the farthest limits of the sea,
even there your hand shall lead me,
and your right hand shall hold me fast. (Ps 139:7-10)

As a people whose God discovered them everywhere, their prayer traditions developed before they had a temple. And though they eventually built a temple and settled as a culture, the origins of their relationship to Yahweh as the God they could not walk past, as the God who met them on the way to their future, left them men and women who prayed the prayers of the wanderer forever. Furthermore, although they adapted readily to planting and harvesting grains and vines and these brought them great wealth, their sacrifices of bread and wine could never displace the shepherd's sacrifice of flesh and blood. Bread and wine could only symbolize the greater sacrifice of the man who had no place to lay his head.

One of the first personal prayers recorded in the Bible occurs under a canopy of stars, and it is not praise; rather, it is a complaint. An old man is mad at God for not keeping a promise. He had tossed and turned in his tent that night until God came to him in a vision: "Do not be afraid, Abram, I am your shield; your reward shall be very great."

Abram was in no mood for words of encouragement. He awoke from semiconsciousness to a piqued state of anger. "O Lord GOD, what will you give me, for I continue childless, and the heir of my house is Eliezer of Damascus?"

Abram continued his tirade: "You have given me no offspring, and so a slave born in my house is to be my heir." Then God spoke again: "This man shall not be your heir; no one but your very own issue shall be your heir." Then it says of God that "he brought him outside and said, 'Look toward heaven and count the stars, if you are able to count them.'" Then God to him, "So shall your decendants be." The narrator then tells us of Abram: "And he believed the LORD; and the LORD reckoned it to him as righteousness" (Gen 15:1-6).

God brought Abram out of his tent and showed him the stars. What Abram saw was not an astrological sign but an astronomical metaphor. "Count the stars, if you are able to count them. . . . So shall your descendants be." Abram believed. And it has come true. The descendants of Abraham are uncountable.

For God to break through Abram's nightmarish anger, he woke Abram up with a face full of cool night air, eyes full of stars—then God could talk to him.

King David played the harp and sang, and he fought wars and governed, so his prayers are at once sweet music and hard-bitten. The genius of David was like George Washington and Isaac Watts in one person. Prayer for David was life and death—and art and grace—and he was the best in the world at both. His hymns are true to the steep pitch of life, deep in the workings of the soul and relentlessly God-centered.

David grew in his art as a young shepherd as he experienced God leading him to green pastures and still waters, and as God strengthened him to defeat the lion and the bear. As a man David reflected these memories in a psalm:

Be merciful to me, O God, be merciful to me,
    for in you my soul takes refuge;
in the shadow of your wings I will take refuge,
until the destroying storms pass by. (Ps 57:1)

I lie down among lions
    that greedily devour human prey;
their teeth are spears and arrows,
    their tongues sharp swords. (Ps 57:4)

    Awake, my soul!
Awake, O harp and lyre!
    I will awake the dawn. (Ps 57:8)

For your steadfast love is as high as the heavens;
your faithfulness extends to the clouds. (Ps 57:10)

David's free-flowing prayer of desperation and praise springs
from the physical metaphors of his life of shepherding. His word
pictures of faith ran deeper in him than his troubles. David's
psalms came from prayers he'd prayed and things he'd seen over
many years. He drew upon times he'd seen mother birds shield
their young through a storm, times he'd fought lions, times he'd
played the lyre to the light of the rising sun, and times he'd stared
into the sky, wondering at the height and power of cumulus nimbi.
Thus the Spirit of God prayed through him with metaphors deeper
than words, that is, with pictures in his mind more powerful than
concepts. When Jesus tells us to consider the ravens, he is asking
us to pray like David.

We can barely appreciate the significance of the fact that although David lived in a world in which the surrounding peoples
worshiped sky, clouds, and sun, David learned to pray to his Lord,
Yahweh, the God who created the heavens and the earth, without
worshiping the heavens and the earth, by mediating his direct experience of these spectacular phenomena metaphorically.

David never quotes the first two commandments in any of his
prayers: (1) "You shall have no other gods before me." (2) "You shall
not make for yourself an idol, whether in the form of anything that
is in heaven above, or that is on the earth beneath, or that is in the
water under the earth" (Ex 20:3-4). But David taught Israel how to
pray metaphor pictures of all natural phenomena in ways that not
only avoid breaking the first two commandments but reinforce
their truth. God taught Moses the Shema: "Hear, O Israel: The Lord
is our God, the Lord alone" (Deut 6:4). God taught David how to
pray the Shema: "For God alone my soul waits in silence; from him
comes my salvation. He alone is my rock and my salvation, my for-

tress; I shall never be shaken" (Ps 62:1-2).

Much later, when the Jewish people lived throughout the Mediterranean world, Jewish pilgrims traveled great distances to worship at Jerusalem during the chief festivals. As they traveled, they sang songs to prepare their hearts, to embolden themselves through the dangers of travel, to worship God along the way and probably also to pass the time. Many of these songs are now collected as the Psalms of Ascents. The pilgrims sang these songs as they *ascended* to Jerusalem, which of course is built on a hill. Because of the outstanding significance of Zion as the mountain of God, wherever the pilgrims began and no matter how high the mountain passes they climbed, every step toward Jerusalem was a step of ascent. The Songs of Ascents are among the most beloved psalms in the Scriptures.

> I lift up my eyes to the hills—
>   from where will my help come?
> My help comes from the LORD,
>   who made heaven and earth. (Ps 121:1-2)

> I was glad when they said to me,
>   "Let us go to the house of the LORD!" (Ps 122:1)

> When the LORD restored the fortunes of Zion,
>   we were like those who dream.
> Then our mouth was filled with laughter,
>   and our tongue with shouts of joy. (Ps 126:1-2)

> May those who sow in tears
>   reap with shouts of joy.
> Those who go out weeping,
>   bearing the seed for sowing,
> shall come home with shouts of joy,
>   carrying their sheaves. (Ps 126:5-6)

> Unless the LORD builds the house,
>   those who build it labor in vain.

Unless the LORD guards the city,
   the guard keeps watch in vain. (Ps 127:1)

Here again, even at a time when God's people worshiped in
homes, synagogues and temples, when they were to a large degree
an urban people, they prayed on the move with metaphors of life
drawn from the physical world around them. Undoubtedly along
the way, as they ascended to Jerusalem, they saw ravens at work,
meadows of wild lilies and fields of grass.

All this, and yet we have interpreted prayer as something we do
sitting, standing or kneeling in one place. I dare say that David
himself would have fallen asleep trying to do what we call prayer
for more than ten minutes. Rather, he danced.

The Body Matters in Prayer

The body matters in prayer, as does the physical world around us.
We know this and yet many of us understand prayer as an exercise
in which we should ideally subdue, quiet or otherwise discipline
the body so that it remains dormant while we engage in the spiritual exercise of prayer. There is no question about the fact that
prayer is a spiritual exercise. Prayer is in its very essence our soul
in communion with the Spirit of God. The fallacy lies in the idea
that the body must be subdued in order for the soul to commune
with the Spirit of God. The very term *quiet time* (the fullest term
being *quiet time with God*) implies this very thing—that we go to a
quiet place and quiet the body so that we can be with God in quiet.
Why can't we call it *noisy time*? Why can't we call it *moving time*?
Why can't we say, "I had a great *noisy time* with God this morning."
I know of no biblical mandate for quiet time. For me, quiet time always turns into *sleepy time*. I think what we have been calling quiet
time should really, biblically, be termed *alone time*.

Doesn't Jesus tell us to pray in our prayer closet alone? Indeed.
He tells us, "But whenever you pray, go into your room and shut

the door and pray to your Father who is in secret; and your Father who sees in secret will reward you" (Mt 6:6). Jesus tells us to pray in secret, not in quiet. How quiet would that room be? He was probably referring to the pantry or storage room of a small house. The house filled with children, animals, neighbors and street noise would have provided precious little quiet time. However, alone in the pantry, hearing the glorious cry of a child at play, the parent might well have prayed more fervently for that child than if they had been praying in an insulated room.

Did not Jesus go to the mountain to pray? Absolutely. When did you last pray on a mountain? I prayed on a mountain yesterday, alone. Birds whistled, the river roared, the wind howled, and my heart thumped as I climbed the mountain. Alone with God, I felt quite free to speak out loud. It was not quiet—and my body was not subdued—and my prayers reflected invigoration.

Doesn't it say "Be still, and know that I am God" (Ps 46:10)? Yes, it does. But in the context of Psalm 46 the injunction means "be still" in the presence of war's violent destruction and mountains that are shaking and falling into the heart of the sea. It means to *be still* in the midst of chaos.

Many Christians, including pastors, report difficulty praying for more than ten minutes. Can we do anything for more than ten minutes? Of course. Most of us, whether we will admit it or not, can shop for eight hours. Yes, the same person who cannot pray for more than ten minutes can shop for eight hours. I can shop for clothes for about thirty minutes. But I can spend three hours in a computer store. I can browse four hours in a theological bookstore before my first blink.

We consume for eight hours, and we pray for ten minutes. Or is it that we have construed prayer as something so preposterously body depriving, so mind-numbingly inactive that it is impossible to imagine praying for eight hours and still have a heartbeat? I think that's it. It's easy to say we need to spend more time praying and less time shopping. But this guilt won't help unless we find a physical way to pray more hours. We cannot pray a minute longer than our body allows us. It isn't mind over matter. The brain is matter. The body is matter. The soul isn't matter. But what the body and brain do in prayer does matter to the soul because in this life the soul needs the body and the brain to give it all things human—even in prayer. The soul cannot exult in Handel's *Messiah* without hearing, which is purely a material matter. And the soul cannot enter into the divine commune of prayer without the words and groans and work of the body and the brain. Without the body and the brain in prayer, we cannot think of God in the soul, and the soul will starve in the process.

We pray body and soul and no other way. The body is neither the prison of the soul nor the enemy of prayer, though we have treated it as such. Instead of denying the body in prayer, we must deny bodyless prayer. When the body falls asleep, praying stops. When the body awakens, prayer continues. When the body stays in one place, prayer issues from that place and is affected by the environment of that one place. Prayer issues from the place where we are and is affected by the places the body moves into and out of. To pray for a community, walk through the neighborhoods during prayer. The prayer will be longer because walking keeps the body alert. The prayer will be broader because moving past dwellings, churches, schools and businesses reminds us to pray for persons and community concerns that never would have entered the mind otherwise. The prayer will be deeper because the sum total of the sights and sounds weighs heavy on the soul.

On the other hand, when the prayer is prompted by a central and demanding irritant—the sermon isn't getting anywhere, a child is in trouble, a dear one is sick, we are depressed, the church faces demanding times, we are at a crossroads—then getting out to pray surrounded by many sensory stimulants can keep us focused on the one issue at hand. How can this be?

It is difficult to talk with a friend in a room with a television on. It is not difficult to talk to a friend in an appliance showroom with twenty televisions blazing. It is difficult to read a book in a room where only two people are talking. It is easy to read a book in a café with thirty people talking. Walking and praying in a forest alive with birds, insects, intermittent wind noises blowing through branches and reeds, and gurgling creeks may be intensely focused. Out of the din of forest sounds, the ear is distracted by the sound of a woodpecker cracking away at an old beetle-ridden pine. The trail and the prayer diverge—the woodpecker is considered; the woodpecker pounds his head against a tree to feed; we pound our mind against a problem to solve it; we return to the irritant for prayer more intensely than before.

The Mind Wandering in Prayer

Wandering does matter in prayer. I spend many hours wandering before the Lord in our church building. When the place is quiet, I pace up and down the rows of the sanctuary or in the fellowship hall, speaking to the Lord, not knowing where I am going. Of course I am going nowhere. But I can wander through the church for thirty minutes or several hours, and not only do my body and mind stay awake, but as I walk I am reminded what to pray for. Who needs a prayer list? As I walk by empty classrooms, I pray for the teachers and assistants who teach on Sunday morning and Wednesday night. I walk past a pew. I know who sits there every Sunday, and I pray for them. I see the pulpit. I pray for the ministry of the Word of God. I see the piano. I pray for the music ministry. I see the stained glass dove. I pray for the outpouring of the Holy Spirit upon the congregation. I see a bat. (Yes, several times each summer bats wiggle through the heating vents into our sanctuary.) And I pray, *Lord protect us!* The church building is the best prayer list I could ever have. To pray this prayer list, I must walk through my prayer list. The physical act of wandering in the church multiplies by many times the number of hours I can pray for the church. The reasons are simple. I can stay alert longer walking than sitting, and seeing a piano produces a more graphic influence on my mind than reading "Pray for the music ministry" on a prayer list—thus a more vivid prayer.

Did Abram need to see the stars that night he was bitterly cross with God and ready to give up? We know it was the sight of stars that allowed him to hear the Lord and that "he believed the LORD; and the LORD reckoned it to him as righteousness" (Gen 15:6). Could God have communicated to Abram in another way? What if he'd stayed in his tent? Would he and Sarai have packed up the next morning and headed back home to Ur? Of course we don't know. Would David have prayed the twenty-third psalm if Jesse hadn't sent him out to tend wandering sheep? Definitely not.

Nevertheless, I must admit that the Scriptures understand "to wander" and to be a "wanderer" as something bad. Throughout the Old Testament being a "wanderer" was a curse. As a punishment for killing his brother, God makes Cain "a fugitive and a wanderer on the earth" (Gen 4:12). From Cain's perspective this curse equals a long, slow death penalty: "Cain said to the LORD . . . 'I shall be a fugitive and a wanderer on the earth, and anyone who meets me may kill me'" (Gen 4:13-14). When Israel balked at entering the Promised Land because of their lack of faith, God "made them wander in the wilderness for forty years, until all the generation that had done evil in the sight of the LORD had disappeared" (Num 32:13). In the Promised Land a ceremony designed to remind the Israelites of their humble origins contained the confession "A wandering Aramean was my ancestor" (Deut 26:5). In Hebrew poetry the word *wander* is used in parallel with words like *fugitive* and *beg.*

The Scriptures use the term *wander* metaphorically to depict the specious sins of adultery, idolatry and apostasy. In modern English we also use the word *wander* for adultery, idolatry and apostasy. Furthermore, as we all know, disorderly children wander the halls in schools, pointless sermons wander from topic to topic, and shiftless cowpokes wander the streets lookin' for trouble. No wonder we condemn ourselves when our mind wanders in prayer.

The wandering mind in prayer exasperates Christians, so they quit. Since we've grown up thinking that it is rude and undisciplined to allow our mind to wander when we are at an important task, it is hard to imagine that mind wandering in prayer could be anything but bad. There seems to be no solution. The harder we pull at the reins, the quicker the ornery hoss jumps the fence. Please note: mind wandering in prayer occurs commonly in people who exercise fine discipline in most other areas of their mental life. These people can work at a desk for hours with solid focus, and for them a perfect day off is to lounge in the sun and read a mystery novel in four sittings. They rise early for morning devotions. In nearly all their activities they possess the ability to tell themselves what to think about. Think about work. Think about a novel. Think about a Scripture reading. It's that simple.

To write a book I have to tell myself hundreds of times over several years, "Go to your office and work on that manuscript." So I get out of bed early, walk to my office in the dark and write before the church office opens. When I arrive, I remember that I need to spend some time in the Word and in prayer. So I tell myself to focus on that. Then I start to write. It feels good. But I like playing solitaire on my computer, so I get an urge to play a few rounds. I tell myself, "No, if you get started you won't quit until you win a game, and you don't have time for that." So I resist the desire (usually) and keep writing. My peripheral vision is too good for my own good, so those little pink "While You Were Out" notes scattered over my two desks stick in my eyes like needles. But I resist turning to them, and I keep writing. Thus, a book. If I couldn't tell myself what to think about, I could never write a book. All of us exercise focus in our lives in different arenas. My wife is a school psychologist, and she can concentrate for hours testing and analyzing the thinking processes of the child. A rancher seeds his field in perfectly straight rows while sitting in his tractor hour upon hour with excellent concentration.

But in long prayer our system of focus breaks down—for nearly all of us. It's more difficult than just rejecting the urge to play a hand of solitaire or refocusing on a child assembling a puzzle. When the mind wanders in prayer, it feels as if our attention is swept out to sea by unremitting waves of mental images—and then drowns. There's nothing to return to. It's like waking up after having fallen asleep in the middle of writing a sentence to find that your head fell on a set of keys that erased the file.

Long prayer fails when we try to coerce conscious attention. It seems like it should work, since it works in just about every other area of our lives. Deliberate, conscious attention works for morning devotions. It works when we read the Scriptures. It works when we pray through a list and when we pray extemporaneously and in a group, but it doesn't work for long prayer. Long prayer is just not the same kind of mental activity as other prayer. To pray long, cut your mind some slack. You can't pray long with a choke chain around your frontal lobe.

In long wandering prayer the mind wanders through topics as the body wanders through woods, streets or church halls. That isn't to say that we can never focus our attention on a particular issue during long prayer. Some issues are best dealt with in long prayer. But at any point in the middle of the best long prayer, the most focused theological argument, the most impassioned thanksgiving or most importunate plea, the oddest thoughts can arise, or we can completely lose track of what we are saying to God. We can enter another world for half an hour before we return to the issue we started with, as if nothing intervened. Whatever else it is, prayer is a form of thinking. And most of us are prejudiced against uncontrolled, unfocused thinking. So when in our prayer our thinking becomes uncontrolled and unfocused, we quit, thinking we have gone the way of disorderly children, pointless sermons and shiftless cowpokes.

Can we think of "prayer thinking" in new ways? I wish to suggest that in long wandering prayer our thinking is not uncontrolled. Rather, it is controlled—from our standpoint—by our subconscious faculty of thought generation. This deeper level of thinking becomes the primary locus of prayer. Instead of telling ourselves what to think about, we allow unasked-for thoughts to impinge upon and direct our conscious range of thinking. This frightens us. Most of us do not like the idea of giving up control of our thinking. But that's not exactly what's happening. We simply stop *telling* ourselves what to think in prayer. When we stop telling ourselves what to pray about, then a more primary, less organized resource of thought can transform our prayer. This may sound odd or even frightening. But the truth is that in our everyday lives this is precisely how we talk and laugh and cry with people we really trust. We only control our thoughts around people we do not trust. The result of this shift from conscious control to subconscious control is that deeper aspects of our thinking are released in our conversation with God. In true prayer God draws us into prayer, and God draws prayer out of us. In long wandering prayer, as we let our subconscious generate our thinking in prayer, we open up our vast personal wilderness before God.

How does this happen? When a happenstance glance at sunlight reminds us of God's law, our guilt and our new life in Christ—that's it. A moment later a jet streaming overhead reminds us of a loved one far away, and we pray for him or her. And then we return to our original topic, the one we left the house to pray about—"Lord, help me teach my Sunday school class!" Before long a broken relationship burns in our heart. And then a thanksgiving occurs for what God will do. Then we settle back to the class God has called us to teach and we think through our talk—all in his presence—trying out lines and examples and thinking of possible rejoinders. Then we see a flock of birds flying south, and it makes us wish we were leaving town, but we can't because God has called us here, and the instinct to leave is nothing new, but it comes up again and again, and God is always able to squelch it until it really is time to leave, then back to the class.

Nothing that arises in our mind in long wandering prayer is new to God. Most of it isn't new to us. Still, it sounds dangerous. Who knows what might enter our heads? Are we opening our minds to evil influence? No, it isn't what we think about in God's presence that works in our head for evil, it is what we refuse to think about in God's presence that can destroy us. Is a free-form conversation more dangerous than a lecture? Where did we get the idea that prayer ought to be organized like an essay or a seminar? It is by no means proven that God wants to attend the daylong seminars we hold for him. We politely invite Christ to our tightly controlled lecture, but he sits in the back row with his chair leaned up against the wall making a ruckus, distracting us, wrecking our outline like a rowdy kid taking control of a lesson plan.

He has a hike for us. Leaving rooms and abandoning trails, we climb mountains to precipices too steep for breathing, for prayers too deep for words. The following hiking account by a Wyoming pastor exemplifies this metaphor.

A Prayer Narrative
The trail from Lake Marie zigzags steeply to its intended destina-

tion, the 12,013 foot summit of Medicine Bow Peak in southeast
Wyoming. The hike tires me more than it used to, but I never
tire of the view. Five distinct mountain ranges with summits
above the tree line spread out like points on a compass. The
remnants of the boreal forest, the ubiquitous lodgepole pine in
the lower elevation and the stately Engelmann spruce and sub-
alpine fir in the higher elevation carpet the landscape, save for
the clear-cuts made by the timber companies.

But my hike is no mere nature walk. As I plod, I muse. I meditate. I pray. Long dormant Scripture references bombard my
mind: "Ever since the creation of the world his eternal power
and divine nature, invisible though they are, have been under-
stood and seen through the things he has made. So they are
without excuse" (Rom 1:20).

I get into a "zone" where thoughts of God and conversation
with him come freely, easily. How could they not in such a
beautiful place! I sample in small measure what Moses experienced when "the LORD used to speak to Moses face to face, as
one speaks to a friend" (Ex 33:11).

I finally reach the rock cairn that marks the summit and
hunker down to get out of the wind. I reflect on the God-or-
dained processes that carry on without my permission or control: the massive thunderstorm building to the west in the Platte
River valley, the inexorable erosion of the Medicine Bow Peak
quartzite by the freeze-thaw action of snowmelt. What strikes
me the most, however, is taking place down in the forest. Due to
decades of wild land fire suppression, lodgepole pines grow
thickly, so thickly that the term "dog hair" lodgepole was coined.
Skinny pines no more than a few inches in diameter grow so
closely as to resemble the hair on a dog's back. Yet they stretch
for the sky to capture the sunlight that fuels photosynthesis, the
process that God uses to make the oxygen I breathe. Millions of

trees are doing this, and I have no say or control at all! My hike has again refocused my perspective at least temporarily that life is primarily about God and not me.

As I walk back down to my car, gravity works for me now. My eyes look to the west to glimpse the Park Range Mountains fifty miles distant. Last fall a storm packing hurricane force winds ravaged thousands of acres of old-growth spruce and fir: God's clear-cut. "The voice of the LORD causes the oaks to whirl, and strips the forest bare; and in his temple all say, 'Glory!'" (Ps 29:9).

Most of you, however, probably don't live in such a beautiful place. There is probably no Medicine Bow Peak to climb just out your backdoor. What place does long wandering prayer have for you in everyday life?

Chiseled in native sandstone over the entrance of the arts and sciences auditorium on the University of Wyoming campus is the following inscription: "Prepare for complete living." It's a lie. The quote, attributed to nineteenth century British philosopher and social Darwinist Herbert Spencer, just isn't true. Like most state land-grant universities, "complete living" doesn't include God. As I wander the carefully landscaped U.W. campus, I see monuments to the achievements of men, not to the glory of God. Secular humanism, the favorite whipping boy of the Christian right, is king. What's a Christian to do? Rail against the monolithic nature of the prevailing university worldview and be dismissed as a fighting fundamentalist? Resign ourselves that things will never change and retreat to the Christian holy huddle? Or give ourselves to long wandering prayer?

Acts 17:16-17 states, "While Paul was waiting for them in Athens, he was deeply distressed to see that the city was full of idols. So he argued in the synagogue with the Jews and the devout persons, and also in the marketplace every day with those who happened to be there."

It distresses me that generations of students are indoctrinated into an empty worldview. My response has been to pray and reason and build relationships. I pray, even though it seems futile, that God would put in the hearts and minds of faculty and students a holy dissatisfaction with the status quo. When the opportunity affords itself, I point out the logical fallacies of the university's worldview.

Perhaps most importantly I relate to those that many Christians consider the enemy: professors at this secular humanist institution. We hike together. We fly-fish together. We discuss their current research. We agonize about our children in their various academic and athletic pursuits. I try to dispel whatever caricature they have of a Bible-believing Christian. Undergirding all of this are my stumbling, bumbling efforts at prayer.

You may not battle the giant of secular humanism in a university town, but you have giants that loom as large. Perhaps it is a family member, a work situation, a nagging personal problem. Can we commit utterly, for the long haul, to the God who hears long wandering prayer?

Prayer means nothing if it does not focus on our families. I feel ill suited to be a Christian father and husband. I did not come out of a Christian home nor did I experience having a father growing up. So I pray. I pray like Elisha that my sons would receive a double portion of the Spirit. I pray that, despite outward appearances, they would far exceed their father in godly character and spiritual influence (this won't take much!). For no apparent reason during the day, my children are brought to mind. I take this as a prompting of the Holy Spirit to pray for them.

But no other experience has brought this more into focus than when my son Tim is pitching for his Little League team. Is it just me or is watching your son pitch an exquisite torture? All alone on the mound, my son's actions are in full view of both teams. His success or failure will largely determine the outcome of the game. For days prior to his turn in the rotation, I pray not for victory but that Tim could use his God-given abilities to help his team. When game day arrives, I'm a basket case. The biblical admonition "Be anxious for nothing" seems impossible to obey. During the game I fidget constantly, barely able to watch.

A recent game further illustrates my plight. Tim is pitching against the second place Elks, a team that Kiwanis defeated last time 24-3. Tim starts well, striking out the side in the first inning. In the second an Elks runner reaches third with no outs. Tim works out of the jam with no runs scored. Dad is proud, but as Yankee catcher Yogi Berra said, "It ain't over till it's over." Tim walks the first batter in the bottom of the fifth and is pulled for a relief pitcher. His team is leading the Elks 4-2. A throwing error (not Tim's!) allows the Elks to tie the score, and a solo home run in the bottom of the sixth seals the victory. Kiwanis loses for the first time in 1998. Tim is crushed. So is Dad. He pitched well enough to win but lost.

As we hash over the game later that night, I realize what happened on the baseball diamond was exactly what I prayed for Tim. Doesn't God use adversity, trials, difficulties, loss, defeats as the primary ingredients for Christlike character? I could not duplicate what God took Tim through on that cool June evening. Such is the agony of long wandering prayer.

But part of the joy of prayer is seeing exactly what we pray for answered. Fast-forward to the end of the 1998 Little League season. Tim's team has a one game lead over Oddfellows for first place with one game remaining. A loss by Kiwanis means a tie for the championship. A win, an outright championship. Oddfellows has averaged sixteen runs per game. Their lineup is so big that we call them the "bruise brothers."

And naturally, Tim is pitching for Kiwanis.

I assume my fetal position in the stands, barely able to look. I pray on nearly every pitch. Tim walks two of the first three batters but gets out of the jam by striking out the side. Kiwanis backs Tim's pitching with nine runs. Tim settles into a pitching groove that I have never seen before. His control is great; his velocity is better. Eight "bruise brothers" strike out in the game, four reach on base-on-balls, only one manages a hit. Tim pitches the only shutout for Kiwanis in the 1998 season. To top it off, Tim goes three-for-three, hitting a home run, a double and a single.

After the final out is recorded, I sit in stunned silence, barely comprehending what has happened. Even today, when I think back on that game played under July's beautiful bluebird Wyoming sky, I cry. I thank God for his goodness. But he was no less good on that cool June evening when Tim's team lost the game. Such is the ecstasy of long wandering prayer.

Perhaps there is a long-standing spiritual struggle in your community. I can look out my kitchen window and see a brand-new Mormon church going up in my neighborhood. I like Mormons. Some of them teach my children in public school; others coach my kids in sports. We share many of the same views on social issues. Some of them are my neighbors. I like their emphasis on the family. But when it comes to the ultimate issues of faith, mine and theirs stand in stark contrast. How can a pastor of a small church meeting in a thirty-year-old building compete with a shiny, new Mormon church? I can't. But I can pray. I can pray that God would put in the hearts of people a deep spiritual hunger for himself.

I can pray for those Latter-day Saints people in places of influence that God would touch them with his gospel. And I can rest confidently that God is working, despite the circumstances and outward appearances. I must be in it for the long haul. Such is the hope of long wandering prayer.

My float tube bobs gently on the wind-ruffled surface of Diamond Lake. Fishing has been good. Enough fat rainbow and cutthroat trout have hit my olive conehead woolly bugger fly that I no longer keep track, having slayed the competitive fishing urges one more time. My attention turns to the slowly spiraling group of white pelicans circling the lake. They've picked a good spot. My game and fish biologist friend confirmed what I already know: Diamond Lake is full of fish, enough for both fly fisherman and pelican. But who told the pelicans to come here? Certainly not the clerks at the local fly shop. God did.

I look the other direction at a thunderstorm brewing over Elk Mountain. My fishing day may be over sooner than I want. But God is in control of the thunderstorm. Earlier in my Christian walk I would have dismissed these brooding, meditative times as just daydreaming and a waste of time. No longer. They are the stuff of Paul's imperative "pray without ceasing" (1 Thess 5:17). Apart from these times I do not experience all that God intends for me to encounter in prayer. Such is the promise of long wandering prayer.

Three

Long Wandering Vision

In long wandering prayer, sights on the outside catalyze visions on the inside. When the outer visual environment interacts with the deep structure thinking of long wandering prayer, the result is long wandering vision. Pictures appear as we pray—numerous pictures—pictures of the persons we pray for, pictures of our childhood, pictures of the future, pictures of the future of the persons we pray for. This is visionary thinking in the presence of God. We see the ball on the fairway; we see it landing on the green before we hit it; we see a picture of a sick person we are praying for; we see the congregation as we rehearse a sentence for a sermon we will preach; we see our child—and we pray—we hit the ball—it lands on the green. Do we see these pictures all at once or in a constant stream? I don't know. But we can daydream while we drive a car. A good illustration for point number 3 of a sermon can emerge in a preacher's mind during the sermon—the illustration can be evaluated, shaped and worded while the sermon zips along.

When you pray for someone, do you see a picture of him or her in your mind? Many Christians have never asked themselves this

question. Do you? When you pray for your church, what do you
see in your mind? Do you see different things about your church at
different times? As you pray, do the images shift toward mission?
Christian education? Worship? Do you see conflict? If you pray
long prayers for a church in conflict, you may eventually begin to
see pictures shifting toward healing. This may be a vision from the
Lord or wishful thinking. One day you may be praying for the
church, and unexpectedly you may see a picture of two people rec-
onciled. And you may see how this happens, and you may see
your role in this miracle. This may also be a vision. How will you
know if it is a vision or wishful thinking? It's hard to say. The pictures and visions and dreams of long wandering prayer don't come
labeled. It's risky business. I don't tell people, "I have a vision from
the Lord." Why should I? If the picture I see is a vision from the
Lord, it bears its own authority, and it possesses the power of its
own fulfillment. I tell people all kinds of things I see in my mind.
Some of it is rubbish. Some if it is prophecy. The body of Christ can
discern the visions of Christ. Very often long wandering visions
compel me to think about my life in ways leading to confession, repentance and a frame of mind suited to living in the community of
believers.

We wander through our church building in prayer. Outer sights
cause inner pictures of people and ministries. The inner pictures
come with attached files—memories and feelings. We see a class-
room. We see the teacher in our mind. We see a confrontation with
the teacher two years ago. We see a picture of a similar conflict fif-
teen years earlier with another person in another place. This turns
into a prayer. Lord, let me know where I was wrong so I can better
face the future. Give me wisdom in conflict leadership. Give me
the good sense to be honest when I am wrong. Help me to not give
in to the easy out of taking blame for something that I wasn't at
fault for. Help me never to give in to bullies but always to be kind

to saints in pain. Help me endure the kicks I need, and give me the good sense to walk away from attacks that will only damage me.

More pictures come up, representing more stories, some with happy endings, some with unpleasant results. The confluence of many streams of thought makes me wiser. I see patterns in my behavior. I walk by the same room a week later and praise God for the teacher. The previous associations may not recur. I may instead remember that I led the teacher to Christ.

Thus one of the reasons why some Christians will not spend time in long wandering prayer—outer sights trigger inner pictures, which cause painful self-reflection. Thus one of the reasons why some Christians will not pray the Psalms is that the Psalms are filled with pictures of painful self-reflection. We cannot bear the honesty of the Psalms, and we cannot bear the honesty of long wandering prayer until we learn that honesty before the Lord precedes healing. The psalmists crawl forward toward confession and praise. Long wandering prayer gives us time and space and safety to see painful pictures and think them through in the presence of God. Let us pray with David:

> Search me, O God, and know my heart;
>   test me and know my thoughts.
> See if there is any wicked way in me,
>   and lead me in the way everlasting. (Ps 139:23-24)

David petitions God: search me, test me, know me, see me, lead me. These visual petitions call for visual answers. David wants God to see his soul, and he wants to see what God dredges up. David does not fear knowing his soul in the presence of God; he fears refusing to know his soul in the presence of God. This is why he asks God to search, test, know and see even though he knows perfectly well that God already knows everything about him, past, present and future. He knows that God knows; the difference is that he welcomes God's knowledge. He desires God's audit. Why? Because he wants God to lead him. How can we say we want God to lead us if we don't want God to tell us who we really are? The "deep down" of spiritual discernment is knowing who we are in relation to who God is. If we don't want to know who we are and we refuse to face our past, we cannot distinguish visions from God from the projections of our infantile self.

The fact that in long wandering prayer mental pictures hyperlink unpredictably into long wandering visions makes our experiences, feelings and mental pictures—hitherto unconnected—unite into a more consistent and honest picture of our whole life. The pictures connect, and our stories integrate. We see the events of our lives not as independent units but coordinating into one story. And because the sights in our surroundings create an unpredictable nexus between mental pictures, we aren't writing our story; we are reading our story. But the story is not engraved in stone. Seeing our story in the presence of God, we see renewal. In long wandering vision, seeing our stories become one story in the presence of God, we affirm "that all things work together for good for those who love God, who are called according to his purpose" (Rom 8:28). Or as David says, "Your eyes beheld my unformed substance. In your book were written all the days that were formed for me, when none of them as yet existed" (Ps 139:16). We cannot bear to think these things outside of the presence of God. But in the kingdom we can see things that cannot be known anywhere else—unspeakable things.

By giving our imagination to God in long wandering prayer, we open our lives up to God for making right and setting apart. In long wandering prayer our secrets make themselves available to us, and as we pray through them, we offer them to God. Long wandering prayer does not replace honest conversation with our brothers and sisters. We need to tell our stories and confess our sins to real people. But if honesty with others on the outside doesn't lead to honesty with ourselves on the inside, then the honesty on the outside will never sink deep, and we will never integrate all the stories of our lives. Honest talk with others on a few stories shows us the way to honesty with ourselves on many stories. As we learn to be honest with ourselves, looking at our stories unflinchingly in the presence of God, we can listen to others as well. We can live in forgiveness. Genuine Christian community is not freedom from sin; it is freedom from unforgiveness.

This process of inner and outer honesty is vital to all Christian community. All of the members of the community must know honest, inner dialogue with God in order to know honest outer dialogue in community. Dietrich Bonhoeffer (1906-1945) addressed this issue in his book *Life Together* when he said:

> *Let him who cannot be alone beware of community.* He will only do harm to himself and to the community. Alone you stood before God when he called you; alone you had to answer that call; alone you had to struggle and pray; and alone you will die and give an account to God. You cannot escape from yourself; for God has singled you out. If you refuse to be alone you are rejecting Christ's call to you, and you can have no part in the community of those who are called. . . .
>
> But the reverse is also true: *Let him who is not in community beware of being alone.* Into the community you were called, the call was not meant for you alone; in the community of the called you bear your cross, you struggle, you pray. You are not alone, even in death, and on the Last Day you will be only one member of the great congregation of Jesus Christ. If you scorn the fellowship of the brethren, you reject the call of Jesus Christ, and thus your solitude can only be hurtful to you.[1]

Long wandering prayer is about being alone with ourselves in the presence of God so that we can be in community with others in the presence of God. We cannot be honest with others until we are honest with ourselves, but we cannot be honest with ourselves unless we are forced by others to face our own profound inconsistencies. Long wandering prayer is never enough for life in Christ, nor is it the end of life in Christ. Outside of community, long wandering prayer devolves into delusional behavior that is not prayer in any sense. We must look more closely at the two sides of Bonhoeffer's dialectic that we must be alone to be in community and that we must be in community to be alone.

Being Alone with God So That We Can Be with Others

James, the brother of the Lord, describes the source of much of the conflict in the community of believers.

> Those conflicts and disputes among you, where do they come from? Do they not come from your cravings that are at war within you? You want something and do not have it; so you commit murder. And you covet something and cannot obtain it; so you engage in disputes and conflicts. You do not have, because you do not ask. You ask and do not receive, because you ask wrongly, in order to spend what you get on your pleasures. (Jas 4:1-3)

We gloss over conflict, saying that it arises from differences of opinion, tradition and personality, but most conflict in the church comes from our envy, acquisitiveness, desires and the relentless anxiety that comes from never feeling satisfied in a world fueled by covetousness. Jesus prescribes the medicine for the disease.

> Therefore I tell you, do not worry about your life, what you will eat, or about your body, what you will wear. For life is more than food, and the body more than clothing. Consider the ravens: they neither sow nor reap, they have neither storehouse nor barn, and yet God feeds them. Of how much more value are you than the birds! And can any of you by worrying add a single hour to your span of life? If then you are not able to do so small a thing as that, why do you

worry about the rest? Consider the lilies, how they grow: they neither toil nor spin; yet I tell you, even Solomon in all his glory was
not clothed like one of these. But if God so clothes the grass of the
field, which is alive today and tomorrow is thrown into the oven,
how much more will he clothe you—you of little faith! And do not
keep striving for what you are to eat and what you are to drink, and
do not keep worrying. For it is the nations of the world that strive
after all these things, and your Father knows that you need them.
Instead, strive for his kingdom, and these things will be given to you
as well. (Lk 12:22-31)

The Greek word we translate "consider" is *katanoeō*. The *Theological Dictionary of the New Testament* says of this word, "This
compound intensifies the simple *noeō* [to know]; it means 'to im-
merse oneself in.' This may be in the field of sensory perception,
but critical examination is also denoted, and in literary Greek the
idea is that of apprehension by pondering or studying. In the New
Testament visual perception is usually the point, for example,
scrutiny of an object (Jms. 1:23-24), or the observation of facts or
processes (Lk. 12:24, 27; Rom. 4:19; Acts 7:31-32)."[2] The word also
means "contemplate, observe carefully" and even "fix the eyes of
the spirit upon."[3] Jesus makes a simple, effective analogy: God
cares for the birds, and God cares for you. The psalms say as
much. But Jesus is asking for more than confession of a rational
truth. If considering the ravens and the lilies is to make an im-
pact on our deep-seated anxieties, it must go beyond an abstract
truth we believe; it must become a true contemplation. God's wisdom and will in caring for the ravens and clothing the lilies must
become a personal, experienced reality resident in the center of
our being; it must become part of our subconscious, mental grid.
That doesn't mean that it must go from something rational to irrational; rather it must spread in us from a truth to which we give
assent to a presupposition of our everyday common sense. Surely

this requires spiritual contemplation of birds and flowers—but the reader makes a radical mistake in supposing that sublime trust in God comes from serene contemplation. The only way the contemplation of ravens and lilies can produce the conversion of anxiety and lust into faith and passion is for our anxiety and lust to be on the surface, fighting us tooth and nail when we contemplate the wisdom and love of God in birds and flowers. Did Jesus do this?

Jesus wasn't tainted by sin. But we cannot doubt for a moment that he felt pain, vulnerability and desire—the very stuff of anxiety. The devil tempted him in the wilderness and throughout his life. The temptation Jesus faced and defeated is a great blessing to us. "Because he himself was tested by what he suffered, he is able to help those who are being tested" (Heb 2:18). And "we do not have a high priest who is unable to sympathize with our weaknesses, but we have one who in every respect has been tested as we are, yet without sin" (Heb 4:15).

In facing the vulnerability of his life as the Son of Man with no place to lay his head, the writer of Hebrews goes on to tell us that "In the days of his flesh, Jesus offered up prayers and supplications, with loud cries and tears, to the one who was able to save him from death, and he was heard because of his reverent submission. Although he was a Son, he learned obedience through what he suffered; and having been made perfect, he became the source of eternal salvation for all who obey him" (Heb 5:7-9).

We know that Jesus prayed long, hard prayers in the wilderness, and of course he continued to pray these prayers throughout his life when he went off to pray alone on mountains and in deserted places. Do we even need to wonder whether Jesus saw ravens and wild flowers during his forty days in the wilderness? Can we seriously question whether his eyes fell upon the lilies of the fields during hard prayer? Can we doubt that seeing wildflowers in bloom gave him strength? And he saw dead flowers. Can we doubt that these reminded him that he too was made of dust? Yet even the dead flowers reminded him of his Father's love, for it says in the Psalms:

As a father has compassion for his children,
    so the LORD has compassion for those who fear him.
For he knows how we were made;
    he remembers that we are dust.

As for mortals, their days are like grass;
    they flourish like a flower of the field;
for the wind passes over it, and it is gone,
    and its place knows it no more.
But the steadfast love of the LORD
        is from everlasting to everlasting
    on those who fear him,
    and his righteousness to children's children,
to those who keep his covenant
    and remember to do his commandments. (Ps 103:13-18)

Perhaps the dead flowers ministered his future resurrection to him as much as the flowers in full bloom.

The ravens brought Elijah food in the wilderness. Did the ravens bring Jesus hope in the wilderness? During his wilderness fast he rejected the devil's temptations to glory. The Son of Man, Son of David, knew that he would never dress like Solomon in this life. But perhaps the wildflowers provided him with a vision of his glorious dress in the future kingdom of the resurrection dead, which allowed him to see himself in that glorious dress even as he scrounged his next meal and accepted hand-me-downs from his followers in a world in which giving a person your shirt and coat were major sacrifices.

Before Jesus told us to contemplate the ravens and the lilies, he contemplated the ravens and the lilies in his own struggles with anxiety and temptation. It is precisely anxiety-laden acquisitiveness that keeps us from seeking first the kingdom of God and from denying ourselves, picking up our cross and following him. And it is precisely our unwillingness to deny ourselves and pick up our cross and follow Jesus that keeps us irreconciled and fighting, even in the community of the saints.

This sounds terrible. What a grueling way to follow Jesus and be in community. Who wants to spend hours calling out to God with loud cries and supplications? And yet, Jesus' command is very simple. He tells us to consider the ravens and consider the lilies. Paul doesn't recommend ravens and lilies, he recommends instead "Finally, beloved, whatever is true, whatever is honorable, whatever is just, whatever is pure, whatever is pleasing, whatever is commendable, if there is any excellence and if there is anything worthy of praise, think about these things" (Phil 4:8). In this verse the Greek word we translate "think" is *logizomai*, which means "to reckon" and "calculate," but in this use Bauer, Arndt and Gingrich nuance the word to mean "think (about), consider, ponder, let one's mind dwell on."[4] In this sense *logizomai* is certainly a synonym of *katanoeō*, the word from the saying of Jesus we translate "consider" or "contemplate."

Both Jesus and Paul recommend the contemplation of beauty as an aid to prayer and for the cure of anxiety. Perhaps they are both taking a cue from David, who prayed:

O LORD, our Sovereign,
  how majestic is your name in all the earth!

You have set your glory above the heavens.
  Out of the mouths of babes and infants
you have founded a bulwark because of your foes,
  to silence the enemy and the avenger.

When I look at your heavens, the work of your fingers,

the moon and the stars that you have established;
what are human beings that you are mindful of them,
    mortals that you care for them?

Yet you have made them a little lower than God,
    and crowned them with glory and honor.
You have given them dominion over the works of your hands;
    you have put all things under their feet,
all sheep and oxen,
    and also the beasts of the field,
the birds of the air, and the fish of the sea,
    whatever passes along the paths of the seas.

O LORD, our Sovereign,
    how majestic is your name in all the earth! (Ps 8)

Being in Community So That We Can Be Alone with God

The role of beauty in long prayer cannot be doubted, but it must be questioned. It must be questioned positively and negatively. Positively, nearly everyone that prays for long periods of time prefers to pray in an environment where something is beautiful. Even a person who prays all day in a small room is likely to light a candle or put a flower in a vase. Even people that don't pray all day know that if they were to do so, they would choose to pray in a beautiful place. We may denigrate the role of beauty in long prayer as a crutch, but when we read the psalms, alas, they are not ugly. So we need to ask why beauty assists us in long prayer. On the other hand, beauty also presents dangers to long prayer.

Hazy, spiritualistic-emotional encounters in the natural world can, in a sinister way, furnish us with fraudulent experiences that mimic God's approval. I've never met a man or a woman led to Christ by a trout stream, but I've known many fishers who interpreted the positive experiences of trout fishing as God's message that they didn't need Christ or any institutional religion; they found God alone on the trout stream, and that is enough. But canyons don't remind us of the Ten Commandments, and an ancient cedar springing from the banks of a gently flowing stream doesn't remind us of the cross. Without the teachings of the mother church we cannot hear the Lord in mother nature.

Every one of us wants to believe that if we lived in a better place, we would be better people. We tell ourselves that if we lived in an environment of natural beauty that we would be better at prayer. But this is a denial of our sin. It's worthless guilt to think that we are too lazy to pray, but it is a costly error to think that if we lived in the wilderness, we would pray more, and we would pray better. There is a big difference between praying on vacation and praying where you live. You may find a retreat to a beautiful, quiet place a real benefit to prayer, but when you move there, the advantage wears off. If you can't pray long where you live now, moving won't help you. People who live in rural areas are not more fervent in prayer, more persistent in prayer or deeper in prayer than people who live in busier, less attractive places.

However—without question—an attractive, serene environment aids prayer. Why is this so?

We Don't Need Quiet, We Need Solitude

The truth is, when we aspire to long prayer, most of us do not consciously seek a place of beauty, we seek a place of solitude. But solitude does not mean silence. My church office is quiet, but it is not a place of solitude. The church sanctuary is quiet, and it is a place of solitude. A suburban street may be quieter than the Boston Common—but the Boston Common may offer more solitude. Solitude isn't the lack of people and noise; it is the lack of bother. Even though my office is quiet, the yellow sticky notes and the pink "While You Were Out" notes seem to jump off my desk and into my face while I try to pray. The telephone sits there silent, but for how long? We may hike the wilderness and successfully escape human beings, but a swarm of mosquitoes wrecks prayer. For prayer, feeling a tick crawling in your ear on a hike in the woods is like a vacuum cleaner starting up in a sanctuary; no matter how beautiful the place is, bother destroys meditation. Solitude is escape from harassment—so that we can harass God importunely.

But solitude requires more than nothing. Sensory deprivation disorients the brain. It can literally drive us crazy. If we can't taste, we don't eat. We don't withdraw to the forest for silence. Forests aren't quiet. The sights, sounds, smells and feelings of the forest all contribute to prayer. The forest's positive sensory experience triggers solitude as much as the seclusion. For prayer we want the church sanctuary quiet but not dull. A room lit by a candle may be simple, but the fire upon the taper pours energy into the optic nerve, galvanizing the soul. Typically monasteries are quiet and secluded. But what that really means is that monasteries don't allow yakkety-yak. There may be singing, incense and art. The bulk of monks live surrounded by beautiful scenery, art, gardens, music, liturgy and literature. When they build retreat centers in ugly places, they fill them with art.

Most people find that the experience of solitude in a place devoted to prayer increases with many visits. The joys of solitude grow with time at lovely places we know well like parks, sanctuaries, farm land, lakes, rivers, botanical gardens, golf courses, rose beds and retreat centers. We need familiar splendor—places we know better than our heartaches. We need holy ground on common ground. We need radiance we know well enough to perceive small changes that make all things new. Familiar beauty is subtle, intricate and mysterious compared to the glamorous thud of a first encounter. Knowing the patterns reveals the exceptions, and it is in perceiving tiny differences that beauty becomes personal and ministerial.

A Prayer Narrative

On my fourth climb up Luther's Footstool, a flower caught my eye. I'd never seen it on this trail or on any trail anywhere. Two in our party of four walked past it. I spotted it underneath wild roses. I asked our friend who lived in the area what the flower was. He said, "This is a rare, wild orchid, the mountain lady's slipper, *Cyripedium montanum.* You are among the few who have ever seen this flower. It is rare because it only lives on certain forest hillsides, protected by overhead plants, and its roots require specific soil bacteria. It cannot be transplanted."

Seeing this pale, yellow orchid, shaped like a tiny wooden shoe, under high, wild roses in full pink bloom changed the walk for me. Our two friends were impressed but not as deeply as I was. They were new to the walk and new to Montana. When everything you see is new, it is difficult to experience real solitude and real joy in contemplation because it is hard to make discernment. The first time through a museum it is difficult to pray as you stroll. The twentieth time, the prayer flows easily—and then the discoveries in the pieces really begin—and we feel quiet and blessed.

Certainly we need trips and changes. New walks spawn fresh thoughts on old problems. But long wandering prayer is not about praying on vacation. Spiritual groupies swarm to the retreat of the moment hankering for a mystic jolt, while the garden variety sinner beats his breast in the holy of holies two blocks from his house. Who seeks an idol and who meets God? Who feels human electricity and who feels nothing—but God?

Why Does Beauty Aid in the Experience of Solitude?

We all know that solitude means quiet on the inside. To be alone with God we need that inner quiet. But we also need the right kind of mental and physical stimulation. Anyone who prays walking on a beach knows that the sights, sounds and smells of the ever-moving, living water focuses solitude and stimulates thinking in prayer at the same time. How does an outside environment of beauty aid mental quiet and mental activity?

To help us toward solitude our sensory environment must in some way work to suspend anxiety and desire—the very things that wreck our inner quiet. When this happens, the sensory environment temporarily blocks our ever-present desire to grasp, possess, accomplish, buy, consume, gain, have—so that for a time, the soul becomes empty, lonely and quiet, wanting God.

A beautiful sight or sound, or an exquisite combination of the two, can stimulate the brain and calm the soul by paralyzing covetousness, greed, hunger, lust, anxiety and worry, while catalyzing the mind to think greater thoughts and free the soul to experience the greatness of God with uncommon freedom. Beauty that encounters us in splendorous glory—whether a grape hyacinth poking its violet head through spring snow, Beethoven's Sixth Symphony, a lovely beach, a poem by Emily Dickinson, or cattle on a thousand hills—communicates to our heart that "the earth is the LORD's, and the fulness thereof; the world, and they that dwell therein" (Ps 24:1 KJV). Since true beauty reflects the glory of the Lord, encounters with beauty can mediate an experience with the glory of the Lord that neutralizes anxiety and covetousness, and heads our thinking in the right direction.

On the other hand, incapacitating anxiety and covetousness will not eliminate the particular irritation, anguish, doubt, need, heartache or pain agenda of a long prayer. Removing yourself from the grind of life to a splendid cathedral to petition the Lord importunely for a loved one in dire need does not suspend the pain for the loved one. The splendor of the sanctuary doesn't provide a respite from the pain. You will probably cry in the sanctuary. If you need a diversion through a hard time, go to a movie. Play cards.

Work out. Join a knitting society. You need activities that take your mind off your troubles. But you also need activities that clarify your trouble so you can think about it clearly in the presence of God. An ecology of magnificence does not mollify bitter prayer, it cleanses it. Tangible glory sweeps the skull of self-pity and plugs bubbling lust. Splendor blankets the sparks and clatters of daily life. We need to see the real issues. A vision of sublime light can objectify burdens as relative evils in a world in the hands of an absolute God. Beauty is the metaphor of providence.

Barbecuing the Pastor in Paradise Valley

The experience of beauty as the metaphor of providence can shift rapidly. The soulfulness of a walk on a beach ends when our mind shifts to the cost of beachfront property or when we see a cottage and feel some resentment toward its owners. Following our mind's wanderings in such prayer, the subject becomes covetousness. An art museum may be a good place to pray. The prices on pieces at an art gallery make it a place we can't pray. It's easier to pray in a library than in a bookstore. It's easier to pray in a church than in a house. The issue is ownership. I don't question the right or the desire to own property. But ownership (as well as the lack thereof) creates anxiety. Solitude is, among other things, the alleviation of this anxiety. Bought beauty does not convey transcendence. Ownership is immanence; infinity belongs to God, which we experience as a gift. Owned art makes for good pleasure, creates a kind of calm and feeds hungry artists. But a sanctuary provides solitude because no one owns it, and it can't be bought.

Obviously a home can be a place of prayer. We can meet Jesus in the garden or the pantry. But if you can't pray at a table with a candle in a single-wide trailer, a big house with pretty stuff won't assist you in prayer. If a windowsill of violets can't make you think of heaven, owning vast lawns won't either. As an old rancher friend, Earl Roberts, used to say, "If a man can't be thankful for what he's got, he can't handle any more." After nearly twenty years of observing people move to Montana to buy spectacular property for the purpose of gaining inner peace, I can state unequivocally that pleasure can be purchased, but solitude cannot be bought—unless it is shared.

The Montanans I knew who truly enjoyed the land they owned and found it to be a place where they could find inner peace shared their land with others. No exceptions. They had different ways of sharing their land. Some let all comers hike, fish and hunt, while others had more restrictive methods—but every single one had a way of sharing his or her land with others and was glad to do so. Not sharing your land makes it impossible for your property to be a place of peace and solitude. Art that is not shared goes stale, and sequestered scenery makes a hardened heart harder.

The Paradise Valley of Montana runs the length of the Absarokee Range from Livingston, Montana, to the Mammoth Hot Springs entrance to Yellowstone Park. The Yellowstone River, the longest undammed river in the lower forty-eight states and the rarely disputed queen of fly-fishing rivers, runs down the valley, through some of the prettiest hay country you'll ever see. The name Paradise Valley comes from the scenery, not the fish or the hay. The Absarokee Range rises perpendicularly from the valley floor to stunning snow-capped peaks poking through a mantle of thick timber packed with elk and grizzlies. This is quite simply one of the most beautiful places on earth. Vacationers equate this visual paradise with spiritual and emotional paradise. Nothing could be farther from the truth. There probably isn't a healthy church in the whole valley. Some Christians who live in Montana's beautiful outdoors barbecue their pastors. A veteran pastor with thirty years of sacrificial service, who never needed a book on loving his church, got bounced after twelve years of productive ministry because the

Christians couldn't share. They called him to serve their church because he had a fine record of growth in small churches. But when the growth came, they couldn't share their space or their power with the newcomers. This mature, energetic pastor got two weeks of vacation a year, while his people whined constantly that they never got time off—which was patently untrue. He got no comp time. No matter how many hours he worked, if he took an afternoon off, it counted against his vacation. He left to take a church in an unattractive place where the people loved the Lord and honored ministry. The Christians in Paradise Valley talked a big line about outreach but didn't walk their talk. They said they wanted people to come to Christ, but it was all yakkety-yak.

We know that Christians do this kind of thing everywhere—but in Paradise Valley? These folks rise each morning to the prettiest scenery on earth. Many of them do for work what rich people do on vacation. But they can't share, and they can't be generous, and they can't be kind. Why doesn't the outrageous landscape—a sure testimony of God's generous love—make people more spiritual, more generous and more loving? Instead the people of the church were stingy and ungrateful, and begrudged sharing their valley or their church with anyone. How can a person be parsimonious in paradise? If the very thing that is supposed to remind us of God and provide us with inner peace becomes an idol, then the beauty is a curse, and it leads to all kinds of moral and emotional horrors.

Montana has the second highest suicide rate in the United States—behind Nevada. The Rocky Mountain states have the highest suicide rate of all regions in the United States. Yes, more people per capita commit suicide in Montana than in Los Angeles or New York City. Montanans are experts at being alone. Nearly all of the abiding, insoluble problems in that otherwise delightful culture can be boiled down to Bonhoeffer's *"Let him who is not in community beware of being alone. . . . If you scorn the fellowship of the* brethren, you reject the call of Jesus Christ, and thus your solitude can only be hurtful to you."[5]

Visions in Community

The highest priority for long wandering prayer is the kingdom of God. "Therefore I tell you, do not worry about your life. . . . Instead, strive for his kingdom, and these things will be given to you as well" (Lk 12:22, 31). But in order to be honest servants in the kingdom, we must each walk with God alone. In long wandering prayer we see the stories of our lives connect to become one story but not an isolated story. We see ourselves in community. In worship we confess our faith: "I believe in the Holy Spirit, the holy catholic church, the communion of saints." In long wandering prayer we see our faith in visions of the great church and the fellowship of the followers of Jesus. We cannot pray for God's blessing in our life without praying for God's blessing upon the community to which we belong. We cannot see ourselves correctly as a child of God outside of our vision of the family of God. Here's a surprise: Paul's famous phrase "work out your own salvation with fear and trembling" (Phil 2:12) is in the plural. We cannot work out our salvation alone. We cannot serve Christ alone. And the visions from God we see in prayer when we are alone are often shared by others. Sometimes these are visions of beauty—like seeing an old, weather-beaten sanctuary dressed like Solomon in all his glory—on this side of the resurrection.

The galvanizing was long gone from the rusty nails protruding from the rotten siding of the old church; if you pounded them in, they popped back out. The eighty-year-old wood wouldn't take paint. Since the building lacked insulation, the water in the Christmas tree stand froze each Advent. The water pipes froze a couple of times a winter. The window glass was thicker at the base than at the top. The windows were cracked and shot through. The ceiling tiles bore yellow-veined stains from the leaky roof. We didn't sweep dirt off the steps so much as decomposed concrete.

When I prayed for the church, I did not pray for the building. Pipes and paint were the least of our problems. But as I walked through the woods praying for the ministry of the church, I never saw a broken-down, old church building. Instead I always saw a gleaming white, renovated sanctuary. I did not realize it at the time, but "seeing" the renewed sanctuary was a vision. It was so modest a spiritual phenomenon that I barely even took it into account. It never came tagged "prophecy." At no time did I feel as if I had been given a message from God that we were to renew the sanctuary because I never thought that seeing a pretty building in my mind constituted a vision.

So I never told the church council, "I have had a vision that our sanctuary will be made brand new." Fixing the place up was never our primary agenda. But for whatever reason, the council began to come up with ideas for making improvements, and the money just showed up. We never talked about vision; we just started working.

Over a period of nine years the building became new. A family donated a new roof. We put up new siding, insulated the walls, installed new exterior doors and double-paned windows. We made the building handicap accessible. We poured new walks and steps. We painted the inside. We relandscaped, planted a new sign, and we even insulated the crawl space under the building so the pipes wouldn't freeze. The sanctuary is now the brilliant white building I saw in my long wandering prayers. It's prettier than I saw in prayer. The realization exceeded the vision.

Looking back I realize that the Spirit slipped the vision of a brilliant white church building unpretentiously into my prayers as I prayed long hard prayers for revival from long hard times. This vision comforted me and gave me hope in God, "who gives life to the dead and calls into existence the things that do not exist" (Rom 4:17).

Four

Battering the Heart of God

Dietrich Bonhoeffer taught his students:

> As a witness to Christ, the sermon is a struggle with demons. Every sermon must overcome Satan. Every sermon fights a battle. But this does not occur through the dramatic efforts of the preacher. It happens only through the proclamation of the One who has trodden upon the head of the devil. We usually do not recognize Satan anyway. We do not find him, Christ finds him. The devil departs from him. Satan waits nowhere so for his prey as where the congregation gathers itself. Nothing is more important to him than to hinder Christ's coming to the congregation.[1]

So I go out on Friday afternoons to pray for the coming of the Word of God on Sunday to defeat the devil. I want to preach wet from the drenching in the river where I begged Jesus to defeat the devil.

A Prayer Narrative

The West Gallatin River sprints north out of Yellowstone Park through a narrow canyon. At a place called Gallatin Gateway, it spills into a wide valley and winds its way through the Gal-

latin Valley, north and northwest to its meeting with the small-
er East Gallatin River at Manhattan, Montana. From there it
flows west to Three Forks, Montana. Approximately 120 miles
from its genesis the Gallatin River merges with the Madison
River and the Jefferson River to form the Missouri River. The
trip is far from over. The Missouri River flows northeast, then
southeast to St. Louis, and from there, via the Mississippi River,
to the Gulf of Mexico. A rain drop falling in Yellowstone Park
travels nearly 3,700 miles to the Gulf of Mexico, making the
Missouri-Mississippi drainage the third longest river in the
world after the Nile and the Amazon. I love praying on long
rivers.

In the Gallatin Valley the West Gallatin River is a wide-rang-
ing freestone stream. It pushes through its rocky flood plain in
braids and side channels. Here the river's flood plain ranges
from 100 yards to nearly three-quarters of a mile wide. The Gallatin is not a big river. Forced into a single channel it rarely
stretches more than 150 feet that can be waded.

The flood plain consists of rounded mounds and bars of river
rock, smooth and multicolored, sized from a kidney bean to a human kidney. In addition, a visitor finds long sand bars, patches of
short grasses, chest-high reeds, red willows, cottonwood trees
higher than the river is wide, and many gray snags of flood-piled
tree trunks and limbs, with an occasional tire and silt-filled back-
pack. The cottonwoods provide nest and cover for large birds of
prey: eagles, owls, hawks and blue herons. Beaver signs abound:
red willows cropped sharp at ground level, thirty inch cottonwood trunks gnawed through and knocked over, shallow ruts in
the sand where they drag branches from shore to water. The
dams stack up the small side channels. There are mink, white-
tailed deer, dippers, kingfishers, numerous types of duck and
geese, fox, mice and black bears.

The flood plain flows through ranch land and the ever-increasing subdivisions. If you can get to the flood plain legally, that is, if you can get to it without crossing someone's land, you can walk as far as you want as long as you stay within the flood plain. The Montana Stream Access Law states that any person can walk or fish any stream or river, no matter whose property it flows through, as long as that person stays in the river bed *below* the high water mark. Several ranchers kindly allow me to cross their land to use the river. Once on the flood plain I'm free to walk, fish, pray and wander. I'm usually alone.

As far as the fishing goes, the lower West Gallatin River gets mixed reviews due to its checkered past. It manifests many characteristics of a prolific trout stream and a few fatal ones. The water is clean and cold; that's good. The banks provide the water with organic nutrients in the form of leaves, twigs and grasses. Streams flowing through ranch land insures that the water will not lack nutrients for plant life. Subterranean feeder springs flowing through limestone beds providing minerals. The river has a diverse shape and structure with many speedy riffles, deep slow runs, sharp bends, log snags, boulders and cut banks. All these features provide excellent habitat for trout.

However, the river's flaws are considerable. Our climate is dry and subject to drought. In a summer with no rain, when the high country snow has melted and the irrigation draw is high to keep the crops from baking in hot sun and low humidity, the flow shrinks to a trickle, the water warms to eighty degrees, and the trout die. The ever-shifting channels in the flood plain hurt the lower end of the food chain. Trout need secure bank structure for cover and aquatic insect stability. An established, secure river channel with relatively undisturbed rock structure provides habitat for profuse generations of aquatic insects—trout food. When the river creates new channels each year, shifting wildly over the flood plain, the insects have a difficult time. Bugs don't like clean rocks. They can't eat granite. Most of the insects the trout eat graze on the living slimes that coat the rocks at the bottom of the river. Slimes establish themselves quickly on clean rocks once the water begins to flow over them, but the insects can thrive best where the slime has built up year upon year on rocks in a secure channel. These rocks are as slippery as greased glass to those of us who wade the river in search of trout feeding on insects who've eaten the slime—so I like slimy rocks too. Without established banks the lower West Gallatin River doesn't produce the massive bug hatches that produce prolific trout populations.

But even with its drawbacks, the West Gallatin can be very good fishing.

So I go to the river, and I fish and pray. Am I working or playing? I enjoy it. I usually walk three to five miles in the process. On a good day I'll catch and release ten to twenty nice trout. Meanwhile, as I walk and fish I'm pounding my fist on the vault of heaven, asking God over and over, "How will the devil be defeated by the Word of God this Sunday?" People come to mind, and I pray for them. My sins come before me, and I confess them. I think about my call to ministry: "How long will I be a pastor?" No answer. I think about my call to my particular church: "Should I stay at this church?" No answer. I don't expect an answer. But there is a question to which I do expect an answer, and I don't go home until I know the answer: "How will the devil be defeated by the Word of God this Sunday?" Nothing. Other petitions intervene, but I will not give up on the one I cannot go home without. "Lord, bless him." "Lord, help those two get along." "Jesus protect my children."

I feel taken advantage of by my church. I imagine a mock tirade with the council: "Blah, blah, blah." Of course I'll never say it to them. But the presence of God is the best place to talk through anger. I am grateful for all the things I've said to God and to no one else. I've spent whole days praying through wrong ideas based on faulty presuppositions. It's OK to be wrong before God. I've prayed for hours through blinding emotions, leading to fateful decisions, and come to the end of the day with one true thought: "That's all wrong."

When I write down a story or a train of thought or sometimes even an entire chapter that I eventually discard, I place it in a file called "Scrap." By the end of each writing project the scrap file is sometimes as large as the book. Was the time spent writing the material in the scrap file a waste of time? Not if writing down the wrong ideas forced to me think better thoughts and write better chapters. If a day spent in ugly prayer keeps me from saying something unkind and uncalled for to someone, the day was worth it.

"Jesus, how will the devil be defeated by the Word of God this Sunday?" Nothing.

I start thinking about the river and my church.

The church is open to strangers, like the flood plain but with some qualifications. On the river I walk where I want, but when I come to a house on the bank, I sweat a little. Even if I can't see anyone, I feel watched and resented. It is well known that many landowners don't like the stream access law. People who move to Montana from far away to spend a small fortune on a miniranch and a mansion on the river don't think of fishers as local color. Honestly, I don't think some realtors tell these folks the whole truth. So I have the right to fish, but it makes me uncomfortable knowing that the people in the house wish I wasn't there. I keep walking and fishing but with a little more caution.

Our church can be like that. We provide access. Anyone can

enter. But some areas of the church are a kind of private property. New people can feel watched and resented. Sometimes
the people who stay feel somewhat uncomfortable. I think
about this, and I pray that God would remove the *ownership
barriers* in our church and release new life and positive growth.

Our church wanders like the Gallatin through a wide flood
plain. Twenty-three pastors in the sixty years prior to my arrival
makes a flood-plain church. The streams of life in the church
wind through many channels, over rocks, sand and through
treacherous, high-piled snags. The body of the church can't
seem to establish itself in one channel long enough for genuine,
positive stability. I pray through the church's struggles over
many years. I thank God for the brothers and sisters that have
stayed with the church, keeping it alive, but they need healing.

The church needs me to stay long enough to establish some
"banks." The church needs to settle into a channel. If the people
in the church felt more secure, they would be less wary of out-
siders. They might take greater steps of faith. They would know
God's love. But I can't come in with a bulldozer and smash the
channels of life that exist. I must let the Spirit of God establish
the church within its banks. If I try to force the church into a
new channel—the one I want—then I am extending the problem, and it will be just that much longer until the church knows
that it is loved and protected by God. When they know deep
down that they are loved and protected by God, they will be
kinder to God's agents in the midst—people like me. The church
has trashed some pastors. They tried to throw me overboard, but
I prayed it through. I carried them to the cross week upon week.

Again: "How will the devil be defeated by the Word of God
this Sunday?" Nothing. I get a little feisty.

"Lord, without your Spirit, the sermon will be dead. Unless
Jesus shows up, the devil will have a play day. Whether my ser-

mon is clever or stupid, without your presence it will be worse than nothing. I will fall on my face for you, but I don't want to go up there without you. If you can use a homiletical disaster, I won't be ashamed to be a fool—but I want to know that you will be there with me. That much is fair. Not for my sake. In myself I deserve eternal separation from your love, let alone your presence working in and through the words I speak. But I know, without a doubt, that you love this congregation. More than I know that you died for me, I know that you died for this congregation, and more than I know that you rose from the grave for me, I know that you rose from the grave for them. I may be nothing more than Balaam's ass. I may be an animated rock. But make me a rock animated with the Word of Jesus that bears the Savior Jesus to the heart of the people of God this Sunday.

"Lord bless my ministry in this church. I'm not that great a pastor. There are lots of things I don't do very well. They'd be better off with someone else. I'm way too shy. How long should I stay here? You know I will stay as long as you want. Do not hide your will from me. Give these dear people the pastor they need. If I'm the one, I'll be glad to stay; if not, move me out. But until I leave—give me the Word of God for them. I know that you can bring a famine of the Word of God. Protect us from that. I don't mind the dry times. I don't mind it when for months and sometimes years you seem far away; I fully accept the fact that 'surely thou art a God that hidest thyself' (Is 45:15 KJV). A famine is different. You hide for our good. Spiritual famine is judgment. Even if this congregation deserves judgment, do not judge them in that way. Remember that 'there is now no condemnation for those that are in Christ Jesus' (Rom 8:1).

"Jesus, you know how much my ego is involved in preaching. I want to look good. You know that I preach with mixed motives. Lord, not for me, not because of me, but because you love these people much more than I do—give me a sermon to give to them. I sacrifice my ego to the cross. But for the sake of the people you love, bring the Word of God this Sunday. I know that you love these people, and I know you want them to hear the gospel, so for their sake, not for mine, pour out your Spirit in the Word this Sunday. Pour out your Spirit in the Word, Lord Jesus; pour out your Spirit in the Word . . .

"Lord, just as high water has moved this river around, high waters have moved the church around too. Some of it's good. Lord, I don't want to change the course of the Spirit in our church. I want to follow the course of the Spirit. It is not my place to force this church into a path I want it to take. But I do need to lead. Give me sensitivity to the movement of the Spirit. Help me pastor my church like I fish this river: I fish the river that is here, I follow the channels year after year—some stay the same, others change. Some deep runs have been great fishing for years. Then they change. I need to find the new water where the Spirit has moved the church's ministry like the river moves the fish. Help me Lord to be a good pastor. Lord, how will the devil be defeated by the Word of God this Sunday?"

 My mind wanders back and forth between fishing, the sermon, my family, the church, fishing, conducting mock debates with the church council. Back and forth, fishing, sermon, children, wife, confession, petition, confession, fishing, debating, catching, a book I'm writing—all in God's presence, it is all prayer.

"Lord, how will the devil be defeated by the Word of God this Sunday?"

A small mayfly emerges from beneath the surface of the water. Floating downstream it wriggles free from its nymphal shuck, sprouts wings, sits upright on the skin of the water with its tiny legs; soon it will fly.

A picture of Sunday's Scripture passage emerges in my mind.

I see the story happening. The man who lived in the tombs, delivered of a thousand demons, well and in his right mind, begs Jesus to take him away. The Scripture says, "As he was getting into the boat, the man who had been possessed by demons begged him that he might be with him" (Mk 5:18). The answer is coming. A thesis sprouts wings and sits upright on the skin of my consciousness. I see, hear and feel the answer.

"The devil will be defeated this Sunday by showing them how, in this story, the characters *opposed* to Jesus get what they ask of him, and the one *he loves* does not get what he asks for."

So here's the deal: before he delivers the man, the demons ask Jesus to cast them into the pigs. He grants their request. After the exorcism, when the townspeople gather and see the man in his right mind and the pigs gone, they ask Jesus to leave the region. Jesus immediately prepares to leave. The previously possessed man begs Jesus to let him come with him. "But Jesus refused, and said to him, 'Go home to your friends, and tell them how much the Lord has done for you, and what mercy he has shown you'" (Mk 5:19). The demons get what they ask for. The townspeople get what they ask for—sort of. He left the region as they requested. But he left the healed man with orders to tell his story. So Jesus didn't really leave the town. Jesus stayed in the man's gospel story. Sometimes those who love Jesus don't get what they want. He enjoins us to stay and tell the story so that the people who want Jesus to leave will not be without him.

I have cracked the nut. I know what must be said.

Four hours, five miles, twenty fish, a hundred prayers, one sermon, a calm heart.

Importunity

I love dictionaries because I love words, so I own a lot of dictionaries and look up a lot of words. When I look up a word in a dictionary, I highlight it in yellow so I can find it more easily the next time. I do this because I look up some words over and over. I bump into them again and again. I cannot remember what they mean. Usually these words are in old books or hard books, but one of these words is used as a subheading in a Bible. How odd to have to look up a word in a Bible subheading. The subheading names one of Jesus' parables "The Importunate Widow."

I don't use the word *importune*. Yet the words *importune* and *importunity* describe a necessary quality of prayer taught by Jesus himself. Perhaps we dropped the word because it describes extremely unpleasant people. To be importunate is to be burdensome, troublesomely urgent, unreasonably solicitous, overly persistent in request or demand, and rude.[2] In its crudest connotations, to importune can mean to make immoral or lewd advances.[3] We do not like importunate people. They spoil social engagements. They sour work. Importunate parishioners disturb pastors. We do not seek the importunate as friends, we flee them. But God eagerly desires our importunity in prayer. P. T. Forsyth observed, "Does not Christ set more value upon importunity than on submission?"[4] From the testimony of the words of Jesus we must agree.

In Luke's Gospel, Jesus follows the Lord's Prayer with a story about a man whose need requires him to be obnoxious to a friend.

> Suppose one of you has a friend, and you go to him at midnight and say to him, "Friend, lend me three loaves of bread; for a friend of mine has arrived, and I have nothing to set before him." And he answers from within, "Do not bother me; the door has already been locked, and my children are with me in bed; I cannot get up and give you anything." I tell you, even though he will not get up and give him anything because he is his friend, at least because of his persistence he will get up and give him whatever he needs. (Lk 11:5-8)

Good prayer is like the relentless knocking and insufferable hollering which can raise a household out of bed and put a man to work in the middle of the night. Even though "he who keeps Israel will neither slumber nor sleep" (Ps 121:4), God asks us to pray as though he must be awakened. As Jesus goes on to say in the same passage: "Ask, and it will be given you; search, and you will find; knock, and the door will be opened for you. For everyone who asks receives, and everyone who searches finds, and for everyone who knocks, the door will be opened" (Lk 11:9-10).

In another place Jesus tells a parable about a widow who will not give up in her demand for her legal rights.

> Then Jesus told them a parable about their need to pray always and not to lose heart. He said, "In a certain city there was a judge who neither feared God nor had respect for people. In that city there was a widow who kept coming to him and saying, 'Grant me justice against my opponent.' For a while he refused; but later he said to himself, 'Though I have no fear of God and no respect for anyone, yet because this widow keeps bothering me, I will grant her justice, so that she may not wear me out by continually coming.'" And the Lord said, "Listen to what the unjust judge says. And will not God grant justice to his chosen ones who cry to him day and night? Will he delay long in helping them? I tell you, he will quickly grant justice to them. And yet, when the Son of Man comes, will he find faith on earth?" (Lk 18:1-8)

Obviously, the woman had no money for a bribe and no influential friends or family with which to impress the judge. The only thing the woman could offer the judge was peace and quiet—when he agreed to grant her the justice she deserved.

The woman waited her turn day after day for her opportunity to plead her case. The judge learned to dread her coming. Finally she wore him down. Listen to what the judge says: "Though I have no fear of God and no respect for anyone, yet because this widow keeps bothering me, I will grant her justice, so that she may not wear me out by continually coming." The phrase "so that she may not wear me out by continually coming" comes from boxing! The verb *hypopiazein* means literally to "hit in the eye."[5]

Jesus is not flattering himself in this parable, nor is he flattering us. He tells us to hit God in the eye with our prayers. He makes God into a stubborn judge and us into pugilistic courtroom lawyers. It may seem unworthy of God. But what seems obnoxious may require supreme faith. Though it may be objectionable to box God in our prayers, the opposite, gracious-delicate prayer is often pathetically self-ingratiating, overcourteous and self-rationalizing before the bar of the god of our personal sensibilities.

A stubborn opponent forces us to think. Required by her circumstances to defend herself with words, the woman in Jesus' parable presented the unjust judge with many arguments. We may surmise that the longer he resisted, the sharper her arguments became. Good prayer forces us to do the same. Thus importunate prayer is theological prayer, not for show or bribe but for the matters of life and death.

Did Jesus Pray Importunely?

Jesus tells us to pray importunely. Did he pray importunely? How can we doubt that he did? Is not importune prayer the quintessential human prayer? He was more than human. Was he less than human? In fact, Jesus did pray importunely. He battered the heart of his Father.

The Scriptures tell us of Jesus, "In the morning, while it was still very dark, he got up and went out to a deserted place, and there he prayed" (Mk 1:35). We can be sure that his prayers were as broad in scope as the prayers in the Psalms. There can be no doubt that he grew up praying the Psalms and that he did so throughout his life. The Psalms were the hymnbook in the synagogue and the prayer book of the godly. Dietrich Bonhoeffer declares that "the *Man* Jesus Christ, to whom no affliction, no ill, no suffering is alien and who yet was the wholly innocent and righteous one, is praying in the Psalter through the mouth of his Church. The Psalter is the prayer book of Jesus Christ in the truest sense of the word. He prayed the Psalter and now it has become his prayer for all time."[6] He prayed the whole praise and pain of the psalms including the importunity.

Furthermore, the writer of Hebrews tell us that "in the days of his flesh, Jesus offered up prayers and supplications, with loud cries and tears, to the one who was able to save him from death, and he was heard because of his reverent submission" (Heb 5:7).

We can hardly hear it enough. "Jesus offered up prayers and supplications, with loud cries and tears, to the one who was able to save him from death." Why, when we pray this way, do we feel it as a failure?

When Jesus taught us to pray he placed before us a selection of petitions:

Our Father in heaven,
hallowed be your name.
Your kingdom come.
Your will be done,
    on earth as it is in heaven.
Give us this day our daily bread.
And forgive us our debts,
    as we also have forgiven our debtors.
And do not bring us to the time of trial,
    but rescue us from the evil one. (Mt 6:9-13)

Of course he prayed these petitions in his own prayers. Are not each of these petitions opportunities for importunity?

Theological Arguments with God

Abraham prayed importunely over Sodom and Gomorrah:

Abraham came near [to the Lord] and said, "Will you indeed sweep away the righteous with the wicked? Suppose there are fifty righteous within the city; will you then sweep away the place and not forgive it for the fifty righteous who are in it? Far be it from you to do such a thing, to slay the righteous with the wicked, so that the righteous fare as the wicked! Far be that from you! Shall not the Judge of all the earth do what is just?" And the LORD said, "If I find at Sodom fifty righteous in the city, I will forgive the whole place for their sake." Abraham answered, "Let me take it upon myself to speak to the Lord, I who am but dust and ashes. Suppose five of the fifty righteous are lacking? Will you destroy the whole city for lack of five?" And he said, "I will not destroy it if I find forty-five there." Again he spoke to him, "Suppose forty are found there." He answered, "For the sake of forty I will not do it." Then he said, "Oh do not let the Lord be angry if I speak. Suppose thirty are found there." He answered, "I will not do it, if I find thirty there." He said, "Let me take it upon myself to speak to the Lord. Suppose twenty are found there." He answered, "For the sake of twenty I will not destroy it." Then he said, "Oh do not let the Lord be angry if I speak just once more. Suppose ten are found there." He answered, "For the sake of ten I will not destroy it." And the LORD went his way, when he had finished speaking to Abraham; and Abraham returned to his place. (Gen 18:22-33)

Abraham comes at the Lord again and again, asking for more and more, basing his requests upon the Lord's righteousness. What did Abraham's persistence accomplish? He didn't save Sodom; there weren't ten righteous people in the city. Did he change God's mind? (What would it mean to change God's mind?) Did God change Abraham's mind? Before praying Abraham was lathered up over Sodom on the brink of brimstone, but by the end of the prayer he seems satisfied that the Lord would act consistent with his own righteousness. Was that ever in doubt? The few pathetic, righteous people in Sodom (Abraham's kin) were saved. Abraham did not change God's intention to act consistently with his nature. Only we need such encouragement.

Rather, in his attempt to move God, Abraham moved into God's space. In his prayer Abraham performed the quintessential theological act—he transported himself into the sphere of the living comprehension, for a moment, of the sovereignty of God, not by titanic analysis but by tenacious wrestling. Did Abraham talk himself into accepting what God had already decided to do? An affirmative answer leads ultimately to the secularization of prayer as self-therapy. The difference lies in the risk of the encounter. Abraham pressed the Lord in person, fully aware of the risk of engagement. Abraham's importunity is like Esther's impertinence. Abraham bargained with God without permission, just as Esther appeared before Xerxes without invitation. Esther changed Xerxes' mind with her facts and her appeal. Her facts were true, but Xerxes only listened because he loved Esther. The Lord listened to Abraham because he loved him. Esther wanted to save her helpless people. Abraham wanted to save his pathetic nephew. Both received the answer they desired. Esther altered Xerxes' course. Did Abraham alter God's course? This must remain an open question.

Prayer cannot turn God, yet prayer must turn God. We know this much: Jesus teaches us to pray as if prayer changes everything, and tough prayer changes more than passive prayer. Surely Jesus' encounter with the Canaanite woman is a model of prayer.

Jesus left that place and went away to the district of Tyre and Sidon. Just then a Canaanite woman from that region came out and started shouting, "Have mercy on me, Lord, Son of David; my daughter is tormented by a demon." But he did not answer her at all. And his disciples came and urged him, saying, "Send her away, for she keeps shouting after us." He answered, "I was sent only to the lost sheep of the house of Israel." But she came and knelt before him, saying, "Lord, help me." He answered, "It is not fair to take the children's food and throw it to the dogs." She said, "Yes,

Lord, yet even the dogs eat the crumbs that fall from their masters' table." Then Jesus answered her, "Woman, great is your faith! Let it be done for you as you wish." And her daughter was healed instantly. (Mt 15:21-28)

What did Jesus mean by this? He treated the woman rudely. And yet when she rebutted him forthrightly and intelligently, he showered her with admiration and healed her daughter. The woman received more than she hard-bargained for. He healed her too. Any guilt she may have held that she had caused her daughter's demonization vanished. Jesus badgered her into his sovereign space—he forced her to take the kingdom by force. The healing was his work, as was his importunate pressure on her to enter the healing process. He became her Lord, not her hero; her Messiah, not her angel. She left feeling smart.

The Puritan genius Thomas Goodwin (1600-1679) gives us a bold example of theological importunity in prayer. Its boldness seems preposterous, or . . . it makes our half-hearted prayers for mercy seem preposterous.

> Turn all thou hast heard or read about reconciliation on his part into motives and arguments to move him to shew mercy unto thee. Tell him it is true, it is in his power to shew his justice on thee if he will, and that thou art freely come to present thy naked breast to him as a butt that deserves to be shot at, and he might desire to spend his arrows on thy hateful soul, or sheath his sword in it; only desire him to remember, before he doth it, that it is the same sword which he once thrust into his Son's bowels, when it pleased him to "put him to grief, and make his soul an offering for sin." And when thou has said it, shut thine eyes and trust him.[7]

Importunity demands industry. Arguing requires thinking. Importunate prayer is theological work. The English hymn writer Isaac Watts (1674-1748) counsels theologically sophisticated importunate prayer. Watts tells us to argue our case with reasons drawn from God's own nature and covenants. He says:

1. We may plead with God from the greatness of our wants, our dangers, or our sorrows; whether they relate to the soul or the body, to this life or the life to come, to ourselves or those for whom we pray. "My sorrows, O Lord, are such as overpress me, and endanger my dishonoring of Thy name and Thy Gospel."

2. The several perfections of the nature of God are another head of arguments in prayer. "For thy mercies' sake O Lord, save me; thy lovingkindness is infinite, let this infinite lovingkindness be displayed in my salvation."

3. Another argument in pleading with God may be drawn from the several relations in which God stands unto men, particularly to his own people. "Lord, Thou art my Creator, wilt thou not have a desire to the to the work of thine hands? . . . Thou art my Governor and my King; to whom should I fly for protection but to Thee?"

4. The various and particular promises of the covenant of grace are another rank of arguments to use in prayer. "Enlighten me, O Lord, and pardon me, and sanctify my soul; and bestow grace and glory upon me according to that word of Thy promise on which Thou hast caused me to hope."

5. The name and honor of God in the world is another powerful argument. "What wilt thou do for Thy great name, if Israel be cut off or perish?" (Josh 7:9)

6. Former experiences of ourselves and others are another set of arguments to make use of in prayer. Our Lord Jesus Christ in that prophetical psalm, Psalm 22:5, is represented as using this argument: "Our fathers cried unto Thee, O Lord, and were delivered, they trusted in Thee, and they were not confounded."

7. The most powerful and most prevailing argument is the name and mediation of our Lord Jesus Christ. "Father we would willingly ask Thee for nothing, but what Thy Son already asks Thee for: we would willingly request nothing at Thine hands, but what Thine own Son requests before us: Look upon the Lamb, as He had been slain, in the midst of the throne: look upon his pure and perfect righteousness, and that blood with which our High Priest is entered into the highest heavens, and in which for ever He appears before Thee

to make intercession; and let every blessing be bestowed upon us, which that blood did purchase, and which that great, that infinite Petitioner pleads for at Thy right hand. What canst thou deny Thine own Son? for He hath told us, that Thou hearest Him always. For the sake of that Son of Thy love, deny us not."[8]

Show this list to an adult Sunday school class and howls will arise that simple prayers are best. The comment that we ought to think as much about prayer as we do about investments and football pools ought to quiet them for a bit. The point is not merely rhetorical. We pray by grace from God's side and simplicity from ours, but simplicity is unmixed love, not thoughtless talk.

God does not require polished theology or flawless faith in prayer. But God may well require a total outpouring of body, mind and soul in prayer as the act of loving him with our body, mind and soul. Simplicity in prayer means withholding nothing in prayer. Long, importunate prayer requires forcing immense masses of dense mental energy through the fine grid that separates our subconscious from our conscious thinking. Where does the strength come from to force our own mental energy from one region of thinking to another? Where does the courage come to do this? What can throw a net into the dark sea of our thinking and drag us up? Only the Spirit of God can do this. Often the Spirit engages us in an argument. It can feel like a life-and-death struggle.

Importunate prayer is not a sign of pride. It is a sign that our pride is dust. Importunity turns our souls inside out. We learn what we really think as the Spirit dredges deep. Importunity calls forth all that we are, places it upon the altar, and we become a living sacrifice. The apostle Paul's admonition, "present your bodies as a living sacrifice, holy and acceptable to God, which is your spiritual worship" (Rom 12:1), cannot be fulfilled in short prayer filtered by definitions of cultured courtesy. Only prayer that demands the last gram of strength completes the sacrifice. We see the ram in the brush at the top of the mountain when our soul is lashed to the sticks.

Life Together

In his book *Life Together* Dietrich Bonhoeffer writes:

> A Christian fellowship lives and exists by the intercession of its members for one another, or it collapses. I can no longer condemn or hate a brother for whom I pray no matter how much trouble he causes me. His face, that hitherto may have been strange and intolerable to me, is transformed in intercession into the countenance of a brother for whom Christ died, the face of a forgiven sinner. This is a happy discovery of the Christian who begins to pray for others. There is no dislike, no personal tension, no estrangement that cannot be overcome by intercession as far as our side of it is concerned. Intercessory prayer is the purifying bath into which the individual and the fellowship must enter every day. The struggle we undergo with our brother in intercession may be a hard one, but the struggle has the promise that it will gain its goal.
>
> How does this happen? Intercession means no more than to bring our brother into the presence of God, to see him under the cross of Jesus as a poor human being and sinner in need of grace. Then everything in him that repels us falls away; we see him in all his destitution and need. His need and his sin become so heavy and oppressive that we feel them as our own, and we can do nothing else but pray: Lord do Thou, Thou alone, deal with him according to Thy severity and Thy goodness. To make intercession means to grant our brother the same right that we have received, namely, to stand before Christ and share in his mercy.[9]

How do we bring our brother and sister in Christ into the presence of God? How do we bring a church into the presence of God? Praying in short bursts may work throughout a working day. But the prayer Bonhoeffer describes takes time. Burst prayers undergird something longer, deeper and more profound or they are of little value. Why? Does God time our prayers and answer only those long enough to deserve serious attention? Or is it because in our prayer God works on us as well as those we pray for? If God means to work on us in our prayers, that is, if the divine-human relationship developed in our prayer is part of the point of prayer, then it ought to be obvious that prayer for our tangled, defeated relationships with our brothers and sisters in Christ will require marathonic prayers. If praying for a brother or sister in Christ will change us—during the very act of prayer—then such prayer must be frustrating enough to make us dissatisfied with all of our previous solutions—the self-heroic, self-satisfying solutions. This prayer must be theological enough to allow us to pray correctly—which means that we will need to repeat ourselves many times until we get it right. Is God waiting for the right words like an eternal Fussbudget? Do we need to get the words right for our own good or for the good of the one we pray for? For the reconciliations we pray for to last, their endurance must be grounded in the good thinking required by good prayer. Do we need good theology to pray, or do we need good prayer to understand and live by the instruction of good theology? If good theology is only good if it is lived out, can it ever be lived out if it is not prayed through?

Our prayers for one another could be shorter if we were better people. Prayer in its essence is simple, as God is simple, because God is holy. Our prayers for our relationships are complex because our bonds are not holy. We pray through our associations from the complexity of irreconciliation to the simplicity of forgiveness and new life, but only slowly. This takes time, and it requires new ways of thinking and praying. If our previous ideas about relationships were adequate, we would not be in such a mess. We need to pray long. We need to allow our mind to wander in prayer because working toward community through prayer renders new resolutions to previously insoluble problems, but only slowly, and only as we live in practical openness to new convictions about God, ourselves and our friends in Christ.

As a pastor I bring my brothers and sisters before Christ in long prayer. I know from painful experience that these prayers can only be long, arduous prayers. Without them the church cannot survive, let alone thrive. These prayers that demand much of us demand much of God. In these prayers I demand of God what I would not demand of a human for sheer courtesy. In God's presence we may need to remove our shoes and fall on our face, but when the talk begins, we need to get into God's face. The English word for this kind of prayer, *importunate,* is as infrequently used as the prayer it describes. God's concern here seems to be stark honesty, the very thing lacking in so many broken relationships.

Praying Anger

Some days of prayer little good comes to mind. No matter how pleasant a day the Lord has made, I cannot rejoice and be glad in it. Surrounded by a natural environment in which it should be easy to follow the apostle's dictum "Whatever is true, whatever is honorable, whatever is just, whatever is pure, whatever is pleasing, whatever is commendable, if there is any excellence and if there is anything worthy of praise, think about these things" (Phil 4:8), it doesn't happen, and I can't force it to happen. No amount of quiet, wandering or thinking produces the event of an excellent thought. A good fish anaesthetizes but cannot heal. Anger veils the vision of million-year-old rock walls spun and twisted like taffy. As I walk the trail, I can only see my feet. I hesitate to pray because I do not want to face God or my pain. Do we have to get into this now? Can't we talk about something happy? There is much good to dwell upon. Why when I try to establish myself in truth and beauty does bully anger come and push my transcendental pals off the hill so he can beat me up?

Moses prayed on days like this:

Why have you treated your servant so badly? Why have I not found
favor in your sight, that you lay the burden of all this people on me?
Did I conceive all this people? Did I give birth to them, that you
should say to me, "Carry them in your bosom, as a nurse carries a
sucking child," to the land that you promised on oath to their ances-
tors? Where am I to get meat to give to all this people? For they
come weeping to me and say, "Give us meat to eat!" I am not able to
carry all this people alone, for they are too heavy for me. If this is
the way you are going to treat me, put me to death at once—if I have
found favor in your sight—and do not let me see my misery. (Num
11:11-15)

My life is distasteful to me. They claw and scratch one another. I
am a man of peace. Can I solve their trivial, tribal feuds? I possess no
access to their reasoning. I cannot solve what I cannot comprehend.
They will not break their clinch long enough for me to look into their
eyes and say, "Stop!" They cannot live without conflict. With central
nervous systems habituated to the adrenaline of pitched battle, they
grip their grudges as if letting go meant death. Gall junkies forfeit the
gift of the Spirit for souls constipated with hatred.

Jesus said, "Blessed are the peacemakers."

I say, "Harassed to the point of despising their lives are the
peacemakers."

Death sounds quiet. Quitting sounds not merely reasonable but
a positive choice to preserve my life.

"Lord, I find no pleasure in living. I lack desire to live. I'm not
ungrateful. I have few regrets. I'm just sick to death of the foolish
accusations they make of one another. Mistrust deadens our life together. The incessant menial stabs, like workers hoeing the soul in
hell, bleed the body of Christ with innumerable shallow cuts."

My friend tells me to step aside and let them fight, to not get involved. Sometimes it works, sometimes not. Sometimes I need to
step in and settle the issue. "Lord, why don't you put signs on wars:
'Get involved in this one'; 'Don't get involved in that one.' Then I

would know when to risk my life for peace and when to step aside and let the gingham dog and the calico cat eat each other up."

So I fail to count the many at peace? Surely it is true: the few fight and the many are at peace. But the few find me. They dog me relentlessly with finger-pointing half-truths, cries of the end of their world—can I not cast Satan into the lake of fire? I am a man of peace wanting none to perish. I will not perform their evil deeds. Their solution for peace is a recipe for rapacity; their plan is nothing but nothing. Nihilism in the name of Jesus! When will their time come? Can I not convince them to turn before the Lord's Day finds their hands bloody? Have they cut the robe of the Lord's anointed so many times that they are beyond recovery?

If they were not brothers and sisters I could turn away easily. "Lord, you put me here, and you will not let me go. You know that I cannot bear another moment of this life. I despise my life for lack of peace. I want nothing but quiet. Nothing but quiet.

"And yet, you know, as always, I bring before you a people you have given me to shepherd. Their lives are sharp-edged shards of someone meant to be whole and living at peace. I trust and pray that they will someday know that peace by the blood of your Son.

"I do not despise the gift of life; I simply feel no use for it. If you will give me the desire to live for one more day, I will spend this one day at peace with you dear Lord. I will seek to be a man of peace. I make no promises for tomorrow. I give to you those who wish to destroy your peace. I bear them to your cross. Don't give them back to me! You will won't you? What will I do about that? I will love them if you will give me love for them. I long for that love. For what I desire least is to abet the madness."

Five

Worthless Guilt About Things That Don't Apply

Guilt kills prayer. Real guilt kills prayer but so does worthless guilt. Real guilt over real sin makes us hide from God and lie to God. We hear in 1 John:

> If we say that we have no sin, we deceive ourselves, and the truth is not in us. If we confess our sins, he who is faithful and just will forgive us our sins and cleanse us from all unrighteousness. If we say that we have not sinned, we make him a liar, and his word is not in us. (1 Jn 1:8-10)

What God cannot abide is our damnable lie that we do not sin. The sin that kills prayer is the refusal to confess sin. Refusing to confess our sin makes us into double liars. We prove ourselves to be liars, pretending that everything is fine when it isn't. We call God a liar because by skimming over our sin, by refusing to acknowledge the conviction of sin in our hearts—the work of the Spirit and the Word—we deny the testimony of both the Spirit and the Word. The inner testimony of the Spirit and the Word to our conscience concerning our sin is a great gift from God!

A man in his late fifties came to me over and over complaining that he wasn't sure he was a Christian. I knew that he was. He said, "I accepted Christ eight years ago now, but I still sin. I have no evidence of God in my life." One day I said, "Before you were a Christian, did you care at all about your sins?" "No sir," he answered. "Did you even think that what you did was wrong?" "No sir," he answered again. I said, "The Spirit of God bearing witness to your conscience about your sin is an extremely powerful testimony of God's love for you and his presence in your life. Jesus is definitely within you. If he wasn't in your life, you would still be sinning, but you wouldn't care. The fact that you care shows that Jesus is within you." That seemed to solve it for him. Once he began to see the Spirit's conviction of sin as a sign of God's love for him, he began to make headway in his battle against sin. His ability to feel the truth and tell the truth revealed God's work in his life. That was his evidence that he was a Christian.

Do we need to confess every single sin before we can pray? Stop thinking mechanistically. If we couldn't pray about anything else until we confessed every particular transgression, all of our prayers would be very, very long indeed. The problem for prayer is not each particular transgression. In the Lord's Prayer Jesus teaches us to pray: "And forgive us our debts, as we also have forgiven our debtors" (Mt 6:12). General confession suffices for generic sins. We must confess some particular sins, but not all. Confessing every sin would be morbid self-centeredness.

The problem is our hideous duplicity in thinking that we are not rebels. We self-justify the inside while performing the liturgy of grace on the outside, making us moles in the kingdom. By refusing to confess our need for God's grace, the cross becomes anomalous, the blood becomes parochial, and eternal life becomes questionable. Can non-Christians pray? A humble pagan may pray under the rubric "You are not far from the kingdom of God" (Mk 12:34), and the Old Testament Scripture "A bruised reed he will not break, and a dimly burning wick he will not quench; he will faithfully bring forth justice" (Is 42:3). A self-righteous pagan on the other hand prays no better than a self-righteous Christian.

Worthless Guilt Kills Prayer Too

No one said that discerning spirits was easy. Not confessing real sin kills prayer but endless confession of non-sin kills prayer too. In worthless guilt we confess actions and attitudes over and over that aren't wrong. Worthless guilt is spiritual hypochondria. Our prayers bring no improvement to conditions lacking problems. We seek God's grace in vain when we beg for a cure for no disease. We feel impure where there is no impurity. We feel lazy after a hard day's work. We read the Bible as perfectionists instead of as saints. We think of justification as white knuckles and sanctification as inerrancy. In our subconscious the Spirit swings a cane and the Shepherd carries a poker. Every canyon becomes the valley of the shadow of death. Incessant confession generates deepened resentment. Indebtedness for everything checks free prayer for anything.

Grace is inexhaustible not because our sin is endless, but because our God is love. If we bear the Image, our sin has a boundary. Though our sin is detestable, our soul remains remarkable. Saying we do not sin is evil, but saying we can do no good is tragic. Evil makes our prayer judgment. Tragedy makes our prayer pathetic. We prefer the latter to the former only as a stage on the way to freedom. The truth is, "If we say that we have no sin, we deceive ourselves, and the truth is not in us" (1 Jn 1:8). And the truth is, "See what love the Father has given us, that we should be called children of God; and that is what we are" (1 Jn 3:1). Christian freedom is knowing this paradox through long prayer for vital discernment.

A good example of worthless guilt many Christians carry, which strongly impedes long prayer, is the so-called sin of wasting time.

Worthless Guilt over Wasting Time

Is it a sin to waste time? Over and over the Scriptures warn against sloth. The apostle Paul tells us to redeem time. However, wasting time isn't in the Ten Commandments. In the Ten Commandments God orders us to take a day off.

> Remember the sabbath day, and keep it holy. Six days you shall labor and do all your work. But the seventh day is a sabbath to the LORD your God; you shall not do any work—you, your son or your daughter, your male or female slave, your livestock, or the alien resident in your towns. For in six days the LORD made heaven and earth, the sea, and all that is in them, but rested the seventh day; therefore the LORD blessed the sabbath day and consecrated it. (Ex 20:8-11)

Granted, the fourth commandment requires us to keep the day holy, not waste the day. And technically speaking, wasting time means doing something evil with our time. But that isn't what we mean by "wasting time." In the present day, in which we idolize work and health, the term "wasting time" is slang for goofing off. We feel wasteful about anything we do that cannot be construed as work, service, family responsibility or exercise. Sleep is now an extension of work. We regulate our night's sleep by the precise number of hours we must rest to be efficient at work. This makes sleep restless. The hardest work we ever do is to do nothing on our day off. We feel guilty doing nothing.

Worshiping on the Lord's Day is a genuine corollary to "keep it holy." But in truth the commandment itself provides its own qualifying corollary; all it says is, "You shall not do any work." Why does

God spend one of his precious ten ordering us to take a day off? Why didn't he command us to never waste time? Wouldn't the world be a better place if (other) people didn't waste time? The Almighty must have innumerable reasons for ordering us to take a day off, but at least one of them must be that without the command not to work, most of us would always work and never pray. Feeling guilty about goofing off is worthless guilt. We need to waste time.

If we feel guilty about wasting time it will be nearly impossible to pray long wandering prayers because long wandering prayer doesn't look or feel like any kind of work we know about. We watch a woodpecker, and our heart feels trust. We mosey down a beach, pick up a stone, and it becomes a metaphor. We catch a trout, and its colors bring joy. We identify a flower, praise the name of the Lord and listen to a meadowlark. But it doesn't look like work. So we judge ourselves. We think, "Rural people have time for that. Those of us who live in strategic places, who have jobs that count, who bear the burden for the financial health of our society and shoulder the evangelical infrastructure—we do not have time for that." Long wandering prayer doesn't look like work, so we mistrust its worth and devalue the effort. We overtrust work, overvalue talent and think we're something that we're not.

Worthless Guilt over a Measly Attention Span

A long prayer may last an hour, an afternoon, a day or several days, but for many of us thirty minutes—the span of a television comedy—is long prayer. Many of us think we cannot pray long because our attention span is short. However, our short attention span affects our prayers far less than our guilt about our attention span. On this point we need to remind ourselves that "he knows how we were made; he remembers that we are dust" (Ps 103:14). A short attention span does not make us pray short prayers. A short attention span merely makes us refocus more frequently. There's no sin or failure in losing focus and refocusing. We love to complain about our culture's short attention span, but our ranting contributes nothing to prayer. Has anyone proven that Christians pray worse today than before the advent of television? Are we quite sure they prayed longer? We have an impression that Christians prayed longer and better before television, but no one knows for certain. Is the Spirit of God paralyzed by our culture? We find it easy to imagine that previous generations could sit still longer. Were they keener in intellect or habituated to boredom? Why did these very generations flock to movies and sit glued to radios when they became available? Why did they invent the television?

As a pastor I am blessed to be the person in town who gets paid to listen to old people tell stories. For twenty years I have listened to men and women in their seventies, eighties, nineties and hundreds tell their stories. The fact is, many of the stories inspire me, but few make me wish I lived back then. Most are sad stories. Precious few involve prayer. I could probably count on one hand the number of times an old person has told me about reading a great book. Alcoholism and abuse abound. I've heard countless stories of teens leaving home at thirteen and fourteen years old because of bad homes. Huckleberry Finn wasn't the only nineteenth-century lad with a no-good dad. Accounts of great churches are few and far between. They love talking about the Great Depression, but few will admit to the life they lived before 1929. I don't recall ever hearing an older person tell me he or she spent a day praying. Believing that we cannot pray today like saints of old is worthless guilt. It wasn't easier to pray back then. Former times were not more conducive to prayer, and less technological cultures were not simpler or happier.

I lent an older woman in my congregation a book on Dorothy Day by Robert Coles. In reflecting upon Dorothy Day's life she recalled an aunt of hers who in the late twenties was a communist.

"You know," she said, "back in the twenties everyone at the University of Minnesota was either in a fraternity or a sorority—or they were a communist." The hyperbole does not disprove the point. Face it, your grandma and grandpa probably didn't tell you everything they did back then. And when they say that they read more books back then, ask them which ones.

We hypothesize the moral and spiritual superiority of past generations because of our fixation on the sins of our day. Although it is true, for instance, that my grandparents' generation was more circumspect sexually, my grandparents were unrepentant racists. One of my best friends' parents and grandparents were taken from their homes in California during World War II and moved to detention camps for Japanese American citizens. They lost the land and homes they left behind. I'm sure my grandparents thought this was the right thing to do.

Generation bashing is hogwash, and so is generation veneration. Start where you are. If praying for half an hour seems like a long time, don't waste a moment feeling guilty about your supposed lack of discipline. If you can pray a long wandering prayer for thirty minutes, in time you will be able to do the same for an hour and then an afternoon and then a day. If you decide to try long prayer as you read this book (hint), start with thirty minutes or an hour. If thirty minutes stretches you to the limit, straining for an hour will teach you nothing. Work on sixty minutes only when thirty minutes seems inadequate. Don't force long prayer. Pray shorter until your soul demands longer. Allow the appetite to grow. Permit the desire to consume. Let it be hard to turn down. Cherish the shortness of breath as your soul pants for the Spirit. Walk into the breeze till it becomes a gale.

Worthless Guilt over Lack of Faith, Laziness and Boredom

"My faith is weak." Long prayer requires faith. But it doesn't require

better faith than short prayer. Most of us feel our faith is up to short prayers. We take it for granted, for instance, that we have enough faith to pray the Lord's Prayer. Generally speaking we recognize that the better our faith the better our prayer, so we always want more, but it would go way beyond reasonable self-examination to question whether we had enough faith to proceed every time we prayed the Lord's Prayer. Now in some ways long prayer is nothing more than many short prayers linked together. Admittedly, long prayer eventually becomes more than a series of short prayers. But in essence, long prayer is a series of short prayers, just as a book is a series of sentences. And yet when we imagine trying long prayer, we wonder if we have enough faith to last a whole a day.

What do we mean by this? Does it mean that our faith in God's willingness to meet us for a day just isn't there? Or does it mean that we lack the physical resources to muster faith for a day? I suspect the culprit that numbs our faith in long prayer is simple human tiredness. Faith, from the human standpoint, is an intense mental event. Exercising faith burns calories, because the brain burns more calories than any organ of the body. This could be the reason why we feel we have the faith for short prayers but not for long prayers. As an intensely powerful mental event, the faith long prayer requires may be beyond our physical ability on some days. We said earlier that we pray in the body and no other way. A day of faith prayer may leave us as tired as a day of digging fence posts—with blisters on our frontal lobe!

So the guilty complaint that we lack the faith to pray all day may just mean that we are too tired to pray all day. This leads to the next subcategory of worthless guilt related to tiredness.

"I guess I'm just lazy." Since nearly everyone underestimates how much energy prayer takes, nearly all of us think we are too lazy to pray all day. A lazy man won't do the dishes. But if man feels lazy because he can't force himself to run ten miles after a hard day of

work—that is worthless guilt. We think we are too lazy to pray long because we don't realize how much energy it requires. Since we underestimate how much energy long prayer takes, we do not budget enough strength for the task before us. We aren't too lazy to pray long; we just don't take long prayer's physical demands seriously enough. I don't know many lazy Christians. But I know a lot of tired Christians who think they are lazy.

"I'm afraid I'll be bored." Tired Christians tend to be bored Christians. Boredom is a soul problem.[1] But often what we feel as boredom is simply the inability to muster the mental strength to pursue something truly interesting. My wife, Debbie, is a school psychologist. Whenever parents tell her that their child is bored in school, she asks them how much sleep the child gets and if the child eats a good breakfast. She normally hears the answer she expects. If their child were half as brilliant as the parents want to believe, the child would find plenty to do in school. The child is tired. We get bored when we become too tired to pursue the love of life and the love of God.

Long prayer is extremely boring without the energy to pray in faith. The quick answer to the question "How do I know that I am not just talking to myself when I pray?" is this: when we are too tired to exercise faith in prayer (note: *exercise*), then we normally end up talking to ourselves when we pray. Talking to ourselves can be very boring, especially when we don't have enough energy to talk to ourselves about something truly interesting. When you lie in cool grass on a hot summer afternoon, if all you can do is close your eyes and sleep instead of looking up to see the patterns in the clouds roll by, you probably don't have enough energy to pray long. Then again, maybe only children see patterns in clouds. Did I mention that childlike faith takes the energy of a child?

So you probably can't give up television in order to pray long. Naturally, you can't watch television while you pray. But when you're done praying, you can watch television in order to rest.

I've watched television my whole life, and I've been praying for whole days for nearly thirty years. If it disgusts you that a book on prayer rationalizes watching television, then you are a lucky person because there must be a hundred books on prayer written for people like you. On the other hand, if your soul has thirsted for a book on prayer written by a person who has spent thousands of hours watching professional football—then you'll feel right at home here.

If you repudiate television to embrace long prayer, the experiment will probably fail. Television requires little; prayer requires much. If you watch television in the evening because you're exhausted from a hard day's work, don't think you can replace an hour of television with an hour of prayer. You need to rest. Television is daydreaming. Prayer is long division in your head. Lazy people don't attend church where I live. Laziness precludes long prayer, but exhaustion deadens it. Please believe me: expanding time for prayer by sacrificing time for rest won't work.

Instead of giving up things I enjoy for prayer, I give up things I don't enjoy, like yard work. I even sacrifice work I enjoy for prayer. Desperate people can pray tired. Job did. But this isn't about praying for days when you've lost everything, and your life is dangling over the pit. Every Christian can pray long under those circumstances. This book is about praying for hours when life is good enough with twenty million things to do. That's when long prayer requires the greatest sacrifice.

Instead of giving up something you enjoy for long prayer, give up something you dislike for long prayer. That sounds silly. We assume that we spend as little time as possible doing objectionable work. If we didn't have to do it, we wouldn't do it we tell ourselves. However, for most of us, this assumption is quite false. Most of us work too hard at our jobs, and when we aren't working or studying, we work too hard cleaning and fixing our houses, garages and yards. We clean obsessively because the great Northern European Mother God tells us nothing is ever clean. Leaving dirty dishes to pray for two hours dishonors her. We work neurotically because the great Northern European Father God tells us that we never work. Leaving work in time to pray two hours dishonors him. Comp time is for the incompetent. The Northern European Mother God resents Jesus for approving Mary not Martha. The Northern European Father God resents Jesus' critique of the elder son.

If you must mop the dust bunnies before you can walk and pray, the God of Israel isn't telling you that. If working until you can barely walk sounds more important to you than wandering through a wood listening to a mourning dove, then you may be a brazen syncretist.

OK, so you're a tough guy who works harder than anyone. You will make time for prayer by giving up enjoyment because you don't enjoy enjoyment. Giving up rest and pleasure for prayer produces pride and resentment. Pride and resentment do not enhance prayer. If they did, there would be peace in the Middle East. There are too many tough guys in the Middle East and not enough lily sniffers.

Cut down on the amount of mind-dulling, unpleasant work you do for Jesus. The fertility gods of Canaan required self-flagellation. But Jesus says, "Come to me, all you that are weary and are carrying heavy burdens, and I will give you rest. Take my yoke upon you, and learn from me; for I am gentle and humble in heart, and you will find rest for your souls. For my yoke is easy, and my burden is light" (Mt 11:28-30). However, David said, "I will not offer burnt offerings to the LORD my God that cost me nothing" (2 Sam 24:24). If we give up rest and enjoyment for prayer, where is the sacrifice? Shouldn't we make a sacrifice for prayer?

Indeed. No sacrifice, no prayer. What must we sacrifice for

prayer? To pray we must sacrifice self-definition and self-will. To pray we must release our control of our little worlds and our little lives. The Lord's Prayer is about our work not our rest: "Thy will be done," "Give us this day our daily bread." When working hard seems more important than praying hard, then giving up work for prayer is a greater sacrifice than giving up rest for prayer. The sin of working constantly, excluding time for God, deserved a place in the Ten Commandments. We argue against the sabbath command more than all the rest.

Who could ever seriously think that giving up television is a greater sacrifice than giving up work? We define ourselves with our work. We enforce our will upon our world with our work. We establish our reputation with our work. We reach our financial goals with our work. The folks building the tower of Babel couldn't rest for a moment. Aaron did something productive with his time, tooling the golden calf while Moses whiled away the hours on the mountain with God.

Isn't prayer work? And haven't we said the sabbath is for rest? We have not called prayer work. We have said that in prayer we expend energy. The fact is we expend a lot of energy in restful activities that are not work. If we cannot work on the sabbath, can we expend energy on the sabbath? Sabbath is for making holy, and some of these activities involve the expenditure of energy. Otherwise, we need to change our worship to other days! Listening to a sermon tires the hearer. The better the sermon, the more energy it takes to listen. Integrating new ideas into hardened layers of thinking is hard work. Some people don't think new thoughts because it just takes too much energy.

Now as they went on their way, he entered a certain village, where a woman named Martha welcomed him into her home. She had a sister named Mary, who sat at the Lord's feet and listened to what he was saying. But Martha was distracted by her many tasks; so she came to him and asked, "Lord, do you not care that my sister has left me to do all the work by myself? Tell her then to help me." But the Lord answered her, "Martha, Martha, you are worried and distracted by many things; there is need of only one thing. Mary has chosen the better part, which will not be taken away from her." (Lk 10:38-42)

Both Mary and Martha expended energy in their chosen tasks. Martha prepared food; she worked. Mary listened to Jesus, and she received the bread of life. Who was more tired by the end? Mary who listened, or Martha who worked? We answer Martha because she worked. But perhaps Mary was more tired. Which is more tiring, to listen or to speak? Neither in general—what tires us is concentration, whether in speaking or in listening. In that sense, we have every right to wonder if indeed Mary, who did no work, was more tired by the end of the meal. Jesus fed the crowds after his sermons. The question is not who expended the most energy, the question is, who the next day experienced joy in the hope of life? That is the purpose of sabbath. It is also the purpose of long prayer.

All the Marthas of the world will never pray long. Leave your dishes in the sink. Let them set for an hour. Go out and meet the Lord. The following experience reveals how one New England woman made this happen at one of the most frantic points of her life.

A Prayer Narrative

When my children were young, I often found it hard to concentrate in prayer. It was better for me to get outdoors for one of my prayer walks, yet so hard to get away from the house. There were so many demands; I never felt good about leaving so much undone. There was always more laundry to do, more bills to be paid, more calls to be made, another meal to prepare or any number of things to be done. My heart wanted to be with God, but I just couldn't break away from my responsibilities.

I wanted to spend time with the Lord, and I felt his wooing all during the day. I would listen to Christian radio and teaching tapes, hoping to be drawn closer to the Lord by osmosis, but it was not the same as talking to God and listening for his response. I needed to break away from all the busyness, the interruptions and endless tasks to get alone with God. I wanted to just be with him.

I carried so much guilt thinking that I was the only one that had trouble finding those special quiet times. I thought I was the most undisciplined person for not having all my life in order at the same time. During those years I didn't work outside the home, so with all those hours why couldn't I find the time? When I did have those precious moments of peace, I spent most of the time confessing how awful I was for not spending more time with him.

The advice I was given during these difficult years was that I should just pray all the time. Pray when driving, when washing dishes, when doing laundry, when cooking, watching TV or anything else. Then out of that intimacy a continuous dialogue takes place. Yes, but still I longed for time with God away, alone.

My dear husband was more than willing to stay with the children. The barrier was within me. I had to take the urging of the Lord and the offer from my husband and go with it. But I had to walk out the door, away from those I loved, to be with the One I loved. Eventually I learned to get out the door, and my life with God and my life with my family have never been the same.

Once I got out in the cool, crisp fall air, I became aware of the pain in my chest. My heart was heavy that morning with needs of my own and many needs of close friends. I was grieving deeply for the loss of a missing son whom I had not heard from in several months. I could barely put words to my pain. Only tears and groans bore evidence of what raged within. The tall evergreens reverently stood strong for me and kept secret what no man could hear or see as I walked along blinded sometimes from the torrents of tears that gushed from inside. I was alone on that quiet road but every moment sensing that familiar Presence with me. This was a safe place to release my burden.

I began opening my heart to the Lord by telling him the needs of my friends and asking him to heal, counsel and provide for them. I pleaded with him for those who were in desperate marital relationships and for others who were seriously ill. I let him know how I missed my son and committed his care over to him again. For a time I ran out of things to say and quietly walked along exhausted from the prayer work.

The Lord was ready to speak. I could sense him there. The Lord's presence was so close and so strong that I actually looked to see if he had become flesh walking beside me. His words from Matthew 11:28-30 became real to me. He said, "Come to me all you who are weary and burdened, and I will give you rest. Take my yoke upon you and learn from me, for I am gentle and humble in heart, and you will find rest for your souls. For my yoke is easy and my burden is light." He let me know that he was even more concerned for my friends and loved ones and that he was praying along with me for them. It was in that divinely appointed moment when I exchanged my heavy yoke for his tender, caring yoke. My heart became as weightless as a feather in that instant. My back straightened tall like those trees. I knew for sure that he had heard and knew exactly what was needed. I no longer was carrying the burdens of my friends, he was.

I nearly skipped along now. The sun came shining through as songs of praise sprang from my lips. Now I could return to my other world of responsibilities and people, but not alone. I was partnering with the God of all creation. The God who is full of compassion and who intercedes for us.

I know God had arranged to meet me in this secret sanctuary. He was waiting for me there. How would I have coped with my pain if I had not left my to-do list and sought him among the trees?

During my prayer walks I found a release of my spirit that helped me get a perspective on life that had not been there before. I could release my anger when I was especially upset with someone, or I could pour out my disappointments and confusion. I could laugh over things my kids or I had done. I could use this time to replay my life and make some sense out of it. I was so absorbed in existing that I was missing all the meaning. If long prayer is so good, why did I resist it?

When I spend that time with God, I am quieted by his love. I learn to hear his voice. Just as a small child is calmed and made secure by hearing the heartbeat of a parent, we can be nourished by his love during those times set aside just to talk over our situations with him.

The way I finally got out the door to be with the Lord was out of a desperate need to break away, no matter what situation I found myself in, to be with him without any distractions. I wanted to hear his agenda. There are just too many directions our lives can take in any given day. When we come to God, making his time a priority, he enables us to eliminate what does not need to be done now (or ever) and the courage to do what is important to him. This will not happen unless we are abiding in the vine.

What freedom I experienced when this clicked. It seemed that years of things I wanted to talk over with the Lord burst out of me. I had a strong sense that he had been waiting all that time for me to meet with him. I freely opened up my heart to God without any formalities. I let him in all the areas of my heart. I was so healed by these times I found every excuse to get alone with him. Occasionally this has meant letting things go undone. This past Thanksgiving I hosted dinner at my place. I suppose partly because of my prayer time I didn't have time to make my special yeast rolls, though I knew they were a favorite. Instead I prayed that this meal would bring our family closer together in fellowship and love. God showed me it was not so much what I served but his purpose in bringing us together. The results were astounding. He gave us the best-ever time of sharing laughter, stories, puzzles and games. God was there in our living room in the middle of all our fun. He wants us to be relational rather than task-oriented. Those rolls weren't even missed!

For many years I struggled (and still daily have to decide) with this issue of time with God, just as everyone does. We all have to face the fact that it will not just happen when there is enough time. These times must be strategically planned for just as time with my husband, time with my children and time with my friends need to be planned because they are so important.

Guilt About Worthless Guilt

Though we have aspired to pray long because of God's call, we have spurned him over and over. We have dreamed about praying long, but we have dismissed it as impractical. We planned time but did not save energy. We tried it once or twice, failed and never tried it again. Yes, God forgives, but will God listen? Will God let us pray for a day when we have refused his call for years? Are we left leaning on the sill because the window of opportunity is closed?

This question cannot be answered in the abstract. Failure to pray long won't keep us out of heaven. Is it a sin to fail to pray long? Of course not. (Beware of asking this question to resentful mystics who gave up watching pro football for prayer!) However, God need not give us the liberty to pray long in a life devoted to work and no sabbath. If we become habituated to work, God may let us live that way until we die. No one can guarantee that God will allow us to pray long. This is not worthless guilt. It is, however, an abstract question. The answer may go either way. One exemption exists in the heart of God. We need not know if God will listen to us in theory if we pray for that which he loves deeply in particular.

We cannot answer the question "Can I go out and pray all day?" But if the pain of life finally creates in us a penetrating compassion for the lost, for the oppressed, for the sick and dying—we need not ask if God will listen to us for a day if we plead with him over the condition of those he cannot fail to care about. We can presume upon his love for the needy. We can presume upon his love for the body of Christ. We can presume upon his love for the progress of the gospel. And finally, if we are willing to come clean, if we are willing to lay our rebellion and resentment before him, we can presume upon his love for us.

Listen to Jesus. Is it possible to believe that God will refuse this prayer?

Two men went up to the temple to pray, one a Pharisee and the other a tax collector. The Pharisee, standing by himself, was praying thus, "God, I thank you that I am not like other people: thieves, rogues, adulterers, or even like this tax collector. I fast twice a week; I give a tenth of all my income." But the tax collector, standing far off, would not even look up to heaven, but was beating his breast and saying, "God, be merciful to me, a sinner!" I tell you, this man went down to his home justified rather than the other; for all who exalt themselves will be humbled, but all who humble themselves will be exalted. (Lk 18:10-14)

We know that God will hear this prayer. How do we know this? Because Jesus tells this parable? Yes. But even if we did not know this was a parable of Jesus, we still would be forced to believe that

God would hear the tax collector's prayer. Do we know this is true because of Christian theology? Yes. Nevertheless, many who have never heard of Christ or Christian theology would be tempted beyond their power to resist to believe that this parable speaks the truth about God. Of course, the fool who says in his heart "There is no God" will not succumb. But the sinner who knows himself or herself to be the tax collector must so wish this parable to be true, that he or she cannot imagine God not listening to this sinner's prayer. But not because the parable makes sense. In fact, the parable does not make sense. By the end of the parable we find ourselves unable to believe that God will fail to listen to the tax collector.

We cannot bear to believe that God rewards the wicked and spurns the devout. But even deeper, when we hear the Word of God declare otherwise, we cannot fail to believe in the God who hears the plea of the humiliated sinner. In the same way we cannot fail to believe that if we pray the sinner's prayer for a day, that God will not delight to listen to us and answer our pleas with his forgiving presence. We do not know if God will listen to us in general unless we know ourselves to be the tax collector in particular.

So let those of us who have spurned God's invitations for so many years with worthless excuses come before him with our lives as they are and ask for his presence as we confess our sins, declare our unworthiness and drop our worthless guilt about things that do not apply. Let us come to him who calls to us, "Come to me, all who are weary and heavy laden." We can spend any amount of time with Jesus. And ultimately, it is impossible to find a reason not to spend a day with the God in whom we must believe when we hear the Word that he exists in love.

S i x

How Can Something I'm So Bad At Be God's Will for My Life?

Perhaps you have always thought that missionaries found prayer to be a natural part of life. Read on and discover the experience of one American pastor teaching in Lithuania.

A Prayer Narrative

Praying is difficult. It's probably the most difficult thing I do. I don't mean the ceremonial prayers. You know: table prayers or prayers during the weekly Bible study at church. I can do that pretty easily. It's the long prayers that are difficult. The praying that takes the time to go deeply into my heart—and God's heart.

I've tried praying in all the "right" ways, with all the "right" techniques. I've found the right place. Given enough time. Attended to my biorhythm and prayed when I'm most alert and ready. I used Scripture and other books to "prime the pump." Sometimes I go for a walk, having found that walking and praying is a good combination for me. I pray the Psalms. But all too frequently (it's the rule rather than the exception) it seems the ceiling is made of brass: my words seem to bounce back to me, going nowhere. My prayer time concludes, and I determine that I've failed again. *How can something I'm so bad at be God's will for my life?*

I was on retreat, a week alone at a retreat house. A week to sleep, to read and to pray. No agenda. No phone calls. I attended worship each morning. I sat for long hours in the beautiful chapel, sometimes reading, often simply sitting before the Lord. I never found my voice. I never felt that my praying made it, that my words broke through to my Lord. After a week I was well-rested and well-read, and while I had spent many hours in prayer, I went home with the same sense that I had failed. *I'm no good at this,* I thought. *How come praying is so difficult? How come I never quite feel like I get it?*

I've been praying for many years now. It doesn't get any easier. In fact, it often seems to get harder. The longer I pray, the longer I pray *long,* the more I struggle with it. I'm at no risk of losing my amateur status.

When I'm honest, as I look back at my prayer life, what stands out is inability. By now I should be better at it. Lord knows I've put in the time, read the books, tried the techniques and done all the rest. If it's God's will for me, why is it so difficult? If it's God's will, how come I can't get the hang of it? Does my consistent sense of failure suggest that perhaps prayer isn't God's will? *Obviously,* my mind says, *if it were God's will, I would be better at it. Since I'm not, maybe I've missed God's will?*

But the fact that prayer is such a struggle for me demonstrates a number of very helpful things to me—so helpful—sometimes I hope I never get good at prayer.

First, my lack of proficiency and constant struggle to pray forces me to be mindful that prayer, like everything else in my life with Christ, is based on grace. That's another way of saying that it's based on God. I suspect my praying gets worse when I take over, thinking that it's up to me, assuming that prayer is about my technique. But the Scriptures show otherwise. The text I repeatedly return to is in Romans 8, where Paul shows the Christian doctrine of the Trinity. God the Father: "And God, who searches the heart, knows what is the mind of the Spirit, because the Spirit intercedes for the saints according to the will of God" (Rom 8:27). God the Spirit: "Likewise, the Spirit helps us in our weakness, for we do not know how to pray as we ought, but that very Spirit intercedes for us with sighs too deep for words" (Rom 8:26). And God the Son: "Who is to condemn? It is Christ Jesus, who died, yes, who was raised, who is at the right hand of God, who indeed intercedes for us" (Rom 8:34).

The picture is astonishing: God-in-Trinity prays within me, prays for me, understands my prayers even when I'm sure my prayer is bad or worse, for Jesus prays on my behalf as does our Lord the Spirit. Suddenly I get it: there's no such thing as "bad" prayer! When I pray, I'm stepping into something already going on, the ongoing prayer or conversation or communion in the Godhead, between Father, Spirit and Son.

A friend helped me cement this biblical perspective on prayer when he showed me Galatians 2:20. "And it is no longer I who live, but Christ who lives in me. And the life that I now live in the flesh I live by faith in the Son of God, who loved me and gave himself for me." My friend paraphrased the verse this way: "It is no longer I who prays, but Christ who prays in me." Ah! Between Romans and Galatians I got it. These texts, plus a few others, forced me to see the underlying grace that inhabits Christian prayer. My weakness, my "bad" praying, only shoves me back to God and his grace; I can't get past grace, thank God!

Second, coming to terms with my deficiencies in prayer has

given me room to relax. I'm not the sort of person who finds it easy to relax. Aware that my praying is inadequate makes me work harder (or simply quit in discouragement). My paltry prayer, immersed in Romans and Galatians, immersed in grace, becomes something else. I don't struggle quite as much. I can rest, relax—activities that are foreign to my nature and just what my soul most needs.

Third, being bad at prayer has made me examine my definition of *bad*. What if I've been applying the wrong criteria all along? What if I'm thinking about prayer in a backward sort of way, measuring it by my standards and not God's? Maybe my feelings of being inadequate, inefficient, slow and just plain bad are exactly where I am to be, for such feelings serve to keep me dependent on God.

If I said my prayers were good, would God agree? Sometimes I wonder if I were proficient at prayer if I would still be as dependent on God. Would, perhaps, even saying that indicate that I was now farther from God than when, in my self-evaluated badness, I was crying out to him with every bit of energy I have?

Fourth, struggling at prayer seems to be the norm even in Scripture. The psalms show me people who often are just as frustrated at their prayer's end as they were at the beginning. Many of the laments, the prayers of hate, frustration and sadness often end where they began. That's not what I would call "good" prayer. Or is it?

Jesus prayed in the garden. Three times, we're told, he prayed "Let this cup pass." I think Jesus at least would have prayed good prayer, that is, he would have walked away with the answer he wanted, with the result he requested, with the warm sense of having communed with God. Nope. But calling Jesus' prayer "bad" doesn't work either. Maybe my definition needs changing.

Praying is difficult. It's probably the most difficult thing I do. I've decided it's supposed to be, for its very difficulty forces me back to God, reminds me that I'm entirely dependent on God and his grace to even pray at all. Prayer's difficulty pulls me into the very nature of God himself, as Father, Son and Spirit unite to enable my prayer. My failure at praying keeps me from taking the credit. It won't let me pat myself on the back. It won't allow me to go off on my own. I'm forced by the very poverty of my prayers *to cling to God only,* and perhaps that is finally the only definition of good prayer.

Some People Think That Others Have It Easier

Christians who do not pray long because they fail when they try do not know that those who practice long prayer experience the same doomed-attempt feelings. *It must be better for them,* they think. The truth is, it isn't. Most who pray long regularly find their prayers unpretentious and even humiliating. It is embarrassing to spend so much time doing something that feels like nothing. The left hand is hardly tempted to tell the right hand about such paltry offerings. Still, when a fellow believer asks what you did that day, and you tell them simply and honestly that you prayed all day, they imagine that something very different happened to you than happened to them the few times they tried it. They smile approvingly, thinking they can imagine that something great happened, when it really didn't. I don't know how to tell them that I walk around without a destination, talking unconnectedly to an invisible person who answers rarely and then only under the breath. With so many important things to do such as call on a dying man, visit shut-ins, work on a sermon, write a note of encouragement, and so on, taking a day to spend unspectacular time with God seems unpractical to the point of being thoughtless.

The familiar rhetoric "What could be more pleasant than spending time with God?" vulgarizes the cross borne in long prayer. Being with God is often unpleasant, not because God is unpleasant. We are insufferable to ourselves. God desires to be with us. But God will not abide with our illusory personas. We can hide no longer. I should think that when a person begins to pray long, he or she might cry a lot. The horribly painful thing about long prayer is being with our self. To pray we must be with our self! Is long prayer anything more than being with our self? It better be. But it cannot be less than that. Long prayer alone can never be less than being with our self. God will settle for nothing less. Maybe that is why God says so little. Maybe Jesus answers infrequently as he waits for us to say an authentic word. Is our unconfessed sin in the way? Yes, to the extent that our unconfessed sin is our unwillingness to know ourselves honestly. Out of love, Jesus will not give us an answer that justifies the specter we see in the mirror. But he will honor us with his presence for hours and years as we search for our true self, so that we can speak an honest sentence—and be healed.

Could the apostle Paul have prayed:

> that you may have the power to comprehend, with all the saints, what is the breadth and length and height and depth, and to know the love of Christ that surpasses knowledge, so that you may be filled with all the fullness of God. (Eph 3:18-19)

without first having prayed:

> I am of the flesh, sold into slavery under sin. I do not understand my own actions. For I do not do what I want, but I do the very thing I hate. . . . Wretched man that I am! (Rom 7:14-15, 24)

Could Paul have experienced visions and revelations from the Lord without his thorn in the flesh? He does not tell us what the problem was, but he is most clear that he begged the Lord (importunely no doubt) three times (perhaps many times) to release him from this grievous burden. God did not answer this prayer. Paul's read on God's intention is "To keep me from becoming conceited because of these surpassingly great revelations, there was given me a thorn in my flesh" (2 Cor 12:7). But his reasoning advances beyond this. For God told him, "My grace is sufficient for you, for power is made perfect in weakness" (2 Cor 12:9). Paul's conclusion is "For when I am weak, then I am strong" (2 Cor 12:11). It does not matter whether the visions preceded the thorn or the joy in weakness followed the revelations; thorns and weakness and visions and revelations belong together. We only pray well out of weakness. Heartache propels prayer nicely. But the best prayers come from emptiness.

When the soul is empty, and we feel nothing at all, we pray best. This prayer is nothing but faith. There we are, walking along, talking to God, not feeling his presence at all, not sure in any way that anything or anyone divine is present, and we know that our prayers are hotter than a .22 rifle in a field infested with gophers. These prayers do not drift into space. They blast off like red-hot shots out of a Roman candle. You don't feel it. You can't see it or hear it. You may be stumbling forward on a sidewalk pounding on the door of heaven with a grievous burden, and everything is silent from God. Utterly silent. No sensible impression encourages you to continue. No tangible phenomenon hints that God hears—or even exists. That is when the prayer is best. That is good prayer. That is praying in weakness, out of weakness, through weakness, empowered by the unfelt Spirit of the living God.

We pray out of the thorn. These are honest prayers. They are honest because in them we pray as we are. We feel nothing and expect to feel nothing because we have no expectation that we deserve to be heard. Then we are praying without masks. We pray not as saints but as sinners. Then we can be with ourselves. We can only pray well as sinners saved by grace. We pray poorly when we pray as "saved" people (Protestant and Catholic versions of that

concept) whom God really ought to listen to and communicate
with to give us an idea that we are on the right track. We are only
on the right track when we know good and well, deep down and
without a doubt, that we live on the wrong side of the tracks. The
refusal to remove it, God's prerogative to keep us honest by making
our trouble obvious, is a mercy, and it is not severe. It hurts like
crazy, but pain is not condemnation.

Nothing can separate us from the love of God in Christ Jesus,
not even God's hiddenness. "Truly, you are a God who hides himself, O God of Israel, the Savior" (Is 45:15). God hides himself and
no more profoundly than in long prayer. When God hides, we believe. Our only option becomes our profound confession. "Lord, to
whom can we go? You have the words of eternal life" (Jn 6:68).

How does faith carry the day? How can bare faith be enough?

Bare faith is not merely enough; it is the only way to pray. In the
absolute absence of feelings and evidence, when we are face to
face with our sin and inability, when we realize that our best
prayers are bad enough to send us to hell (George Whitefield, 1714-
1770), then our thinking loses its self-confident grounding in the "I
think" and reestablishes itself in God who through his very absence, grounds us graciously in the death and resurrection of
Christ. The Christians we truly admire have done precisely this—
they are almost all longtime Christians and very old humans.

Experiences of God threaten prayer severely! "Experiences
tend to make themselves absolutes. Then they threaten the purity
of faith. Faith has been most severely threatened by its best experiences."[1] Our occasional experiences of God, blessed as they are,
do not point the way to prayer, neither do they point the way to
God. We participate in the life of God in and through faith that
grasps the grace of God in the cross as our only hope. In grasping
the grace of God in the cross of Christ in faith, we grasp not a concept but God. Grasping God's grace in Christ through faith is actu-

ally grasping God. God lets us reach for him, hold him and even comprehend him as we grasp him in faith. Faith in God's grace in Christ is our legitimate response to God's existence. Indeed, "Faith takes God's existence as his being."[2] This means that we do not divide our faith in God into whether God exists and how God exists. God is not a bird in *Peterson's Guide*. God is only objective to our thinking in faith. Truly thinking God and true prayer have the same engine: faith. We can only understand ourselves in that same faith. How else can we bear to know ourselves? Can we face ourselves outside faith in God's grace? Outside faith in God's grace we can only lie to ourselves about ourselves. This becomes more difficult for Christians as the years go on. We cannot accept the fact that we are not fundamentally better people than we were ten years ago. Throughout our lives our bodies change, our habits change, our knowledge changes, our families and our world changes. But God does not change, and the fact that we are rebellious sinners does not change. Taking a single step away from this truth endangers our life in God and our prayers.

Nothing destroys prayer more than thinking we have made progress. We can learn a few methods. We can learn to avoid a few basic pitfalls. We can learn the environments in which our body and mind function better in prayer. But these are of no account in comparison to faith. Methods and insights into prayer are the tar on the bat. The tar helps the grip, but the tar cannot drive the ball over the fence. Faith drives the ball over the fence.

But even faith does not save us. It does not make us right with God, and prayer does not save us, nor does prayer make us right with God. The grace of God saves us. The prayer of faith apprehends grace, and the long prayer of faith lets the relief of salvation sink deep. Long laid wounds need anointing, and chaotic visions need reappointing. Long prayer lets justification sink deep. Long prayer gives grace time within the soul.

Therefore we cannot pray well if we think that long prayer makes us better before God. The longer we pray long, the more convinced we become of this. Long prayer is helpless to save us, and the deeper we know that God loves us even if we do not pray, the better we pray. Given the time and scope that long prayer provides, grace enters the catacombs of the heart and calls visions of ancient terrors out of slumber. To put it in frank terms, many Christians will not pray long for fear of what's in there.

Fear of What's in There

Many Christians will not go out and pray for a day because they fear solitude. They fear solitude because they believe that solitude will not lead to the inner peace they so desperately crave. This fear is well placed. When we are alone, we think thoughts that we do not want to think. But when we are alone in the presence of God, we think thoughts we do not want to think in the presence of the Beloved whom we trust with our fears and with our doubts.

When we pray like a child, any thought may arise.

When my son was nine years old, we were on a father-son walk along the crest of a high bank above the Bitterroot River in Montana. The Bitterroot Range gleamed white and high above us just across the river. The first buttercups bloomed in the thin surface of soil above the still frozen earth beneath. Talking about God seemed like the natural thing to do. He brought the subject up.

"Dad," he said.

"What, Evan?"

"Dad, what if God does not exist?"

I probably blinked and gulped, but I regained my inner composure rather quickly, and I hope that, by the grace of God, I gave him the correct answer. I said, "Well, Evan, I believe that God exists, and I hope that you do to. But in the long run, as you get older, you will have to decide for yourself if you think that God exists." It did not occur to me to suggest the argument of design, the idea that the beauty of the earth testifies to the existence of God. I thank God that I did not. Not that Evan could not have grasped the concept. At the age of seven, on a drive to see a friend ride a bull in a rodeo, he asked me to tell him what inflation was, followed by a question about the difference between capitalism and socialism. I'm glad I didn't use the argument of design because I think it has very little force in the constant presence of great natural beauty. I always found the argument of design to be far more convincing when I lived in big cities. Seeing gorgeous mountains as proof of God's existence is one thing on vacation; it is quite another thing seeing them as proof of God's existence if you live around them every day. It has nothing to do with growing dull to their beauty. It has to do with the fact that constant immersion in spectacular beauty does not fundamentally make people better. The one hundredth story of incest in the shadow of the shining mountains takes away the power of the argument by forcing us to take so much more seriously the problem of evil. The Unabomber mailed his bombs from one of the most beautiful places on earth.

A little boy's honest question about the existence of God just popped out of his mouth. It did not hurt him to ask it, and I am grateful to God that I did not drive it deeper by making it seem to be a shameful thing to think. His question certainly did not hurt God's feelings.

But questions like these exist within us. What if God does not exist? What if everything we believe is wrongheaded foolishness? As the nonbeliever buries the suspicion that God does exist, believers bury the suspicion that God does not exist. So much of the nonbeliever's life hangs upon his or her atheism. The thought that God might exist is too much to bear. So much of the believer's life hangs upon his or her theism. The thought that God might not exist is, again, too much to bear. We attack on the outside what terrorizes on the inside.

Pastoral ministry provides one with endless testimonies to human evil. Within every searing cry for justice is the nagging question about whether there is any justice. We might find it easier to let God distribute justice if we weren't so terrified that God cannot do it because perhaps he does not exist. Our own sin raises the same questions. The problem of evil is not just about what others have done; it is also about what we have done. It is not just about why God did not stop others. It is also about why God did not stop us. It is not just about whether we can forgive others. It is about whether we can forgive ourselves. It is not just about whether we will be attacked. It is about whether we will attack.

Many Christians will not pray long because they fear the intrusion of ideas suggesting that God does not exist and our lives are meaningless. It should be perfectly obvious that if there is a god, but that god does not care about evil or cannot deal with evil, such a god is utterly worthless and is unworthy of another thought, let alone worship. A god that cares less about evil than we do is little better than a demon.

This is why long prayer so often frightens us. We pray and we pray, and we hear nothing; we feel nothing; and instead of having great times with God, we end up face to face with the problem of evil in our own lives. When our time with God raises a compelling argument for atheism, it is no wonder we refuse to pray long. Sometimes it requires nothing more complicated than the question "Why can I spend three hours doing the bills, but I can't pay attention to God for ten minutes?" The question beneath such a question is "Perhaps I cannot pray because prayer is nothing, and perhaps prayer is nothing because God does not exist." This question goads all we do in religion. So-called spiritual experiences do not void the question of God's existence.

Furthermore, the question of God's existence is severe for the Christian because, living in faith, the nonexistence of God is tantamount to the nonexistence of the self. For true faith is "in fact, the self-definition of man in which man, on the basis of his being defined by God, renounces all self-grounding."[3] Renouncing all self-grounding in faith means that if the faith proves to have been faulty—then the self is lost too. To the seasoned Christian the thought of the nonexistence of God is akin to dying; in fact it is a kind of dying. And likewise, we deny the possibility of the nonexistence of God by not placing ourselves in situations where our belief in God may be questioned. The intellectual barbs of the nonbeliever do not threaten us nearly as much as praying for a day and not feeling anything. That is really frightening because it is not about a theory or a proof. God just doesn't seem to be there or listening at all.

Furthermore, prayer takes the issue a step beyond the existence of God because the human act of prayer is the attempt to interact with God. This raises the question of the essence of God. That is, if we believe that God exists, what is this God like? Will this God listen to me? Will this God care about me? Will this God grant my petition? Does this God care at all about the pain and suffering in the world? Will this God stop evil in the world? Will this God stop me from doing the things I do not want to do? Will this God make me a better person if I request this? Will this God heal my broken relationships? Will this God heal my own broken heart?

When we pray and none of this seems to happen, it makes us wonder whether God exists because a God that cannot and will not heal and make right is not worth our attention. If this is the case, we might be better off without a god. And many people have come to this conclusion. The rejection of so much gas that passes as god is not merely reasonable but an act that, though lacking the luster of faith, is not wholly unrelated to genuine human knowing. For most surely, we cannot unbelieve true faith in the true God. The hardest questions from life's bitterest events may unsettle faith, but they cannot destroy it. The more distant God becomes, the dearer faith becomes. Faith thrives in hardship, for it is placed in us for certain knowing in utter darkness. Therefore, we do not need to fear the threat of the nonbeing of God. In fact, we can embrace it.

We may embrace the threat of the nonbeing of God in exactly the same way that we can embrace our own death. First of all, as we all know, the threat of the possibility of death only has power over us as long as we run from it. We can look at the reality of our death squarely in the eye and come away alive. We can think about dying and live. In Jesus Christ we can look forward to dying! We can look at the possibility of the nonexistence of God and not lose our faith. As long we run from the possibility of atheism, we are to some extent under its control. But we can take this one step further and suggest that though we cannot embrace atheism, we can embrace the nonbeing of God, just like we can embrace our own death. Because in the death of Jesus Christ on the cross, God has entered death, nonbeing, hell and nothingness, and has experienced its destructive force and emerged alive. We can embrace our death because God has entered death and won the battle. Therefore, in long prayer when we feel the threat of the nonbeing of God, we can view it not as a threat but as something we can face because we do not need to fear our own death. We do not need to fear our own death because God has already been there and emerged the victor.

This is not to make light of the reality of the intellectual challenge of atheism, nor does it really solve the intellectual challenge of atheism. But in long prayer, for Christians who live in faith already, the threat of the nonexistence of God is in many ways connected with the fear of their own nonexistence. The two are solved together in the death and resurrection of Christ. If the problem is the severe problem of facing one's death, then long wandering prayer is the ideal way to deal with it; the problem cannot be dealt with in short prayers. In some ways, short prayers only prolong the problem, merely sweeping it under the mental carpet. In long wandering prayer, we can in an extended and leisurely fashion learn to accept and even embrace our death. In the process God becomes dearer than ever.

The next time you are out praying and God seems very far away and you feel very lonely, as if perhaps God does not exist, try taking this feeling as a sign that you are dealing with the fear of your own death. Consider then the death of Christ and how in his death God experienced death in the fullest sense and emerged alive, and how in Christ we shall emerge alive as well. I know it isn't easy to do, and it takes time. Hard thinking that takes a lot of time is what long wandering prayer is all about.

The real question of long wandering prayer is not whether God exists but where God exists. Job states our case when he says, "Oh, that I knew where I might find him, that I might come even to his dwelling! I would lay my case before him, and fill my mouth with arguments" (Job 23:3-4). Job has an importunate prayer in mind. He's going to give God a mouthful. But first he has to find him. Where is God?

The Spirit Helps Us in Our Weakness

Paul tells us that "the Spirit helps us in our weakness; for we do not know how to pray as we ought, but that very Spirit intercedes with sighs too deep for words. And God, who searches the heart, knows what is the mind of the Spirit, because the Spirit intercedes for the saints according to the will of God" (Rom 8:26-28). What more could we ask for than this? If when we are weak—when our prayers feel dead—the Spirit is praying for us and through us, then those prayers must be better than the prayers we pray when we feel strong. Our weakest prayers in the Spirit are better than our

142 — LONG WANDERING PRAYER

best prayers when we don't feel the need for the Spirit. Our worst prayers may be our best prayers. How do we know what a good prayer is anyway? Do we know how we sound to God? The prayers of the Spirit must be the best, and the Spirit intervenes when we are weak. This raises the question of how we measure prayer and even how we hear God.

Do we measure prayers by how they feel? We find it easy to answer "Of course not!" But when we go out and try to pray for a day, and we come home defeated because we feel lousy, then every one of us rates our prayers by how we feel. Is the feel of a prayer a measure of the prayer? How can that be true? But if we look closely at prayer from the perspective of faith and weakness—then maybe we really can judge our prayers by our experiences in prayer. If we get it right, maybe we really must judge our prayers by our feelings. Maybe if we judge our prayers right, we learn how to hear God right in prayer.

We find it easy to agree that our best prayers are powered by our best faith. If that is true, then perhaps it is also true that we can judge our prayers by how they feel if we can generally be willing to agree that our best prayers happen when we feel lousy, simply because (1) they require the most faith, and (2) we are promised that the Spirit helps us in our weakness. We can't take this to the point of despising prayer that we enjoy, as if God could never allow us to experience joy as a sign of his presence. Nevertheless, it seems agreeable to say that although we find it difficult to judge our happiest prayers since they may be nothing more than self-congratulations, when we feel as dry as the Gobi Desert and keep praying in sheer faith that the Spirit can make something of them, then we must be praying well.

This opens the question of experiencing God in prayer. As problematic as the issue is, we know that we must be able to affirm the experience of God in prayer in some basic sense in order for our whole prayer life to be true. That is, we may pray for years without feeling God or hearing God, but we cannot pray forever without some minimal divine reassurance that we're getting it right. But how do we experience God in prayer? This is a larger issue in long prayer than in other, shorter types because we really can pray for short periods of time without feeling God's presence without any discomfort. In fact, I doubt if many of us really expect to feel God's presence or to hear God tell us something in short prayers. Not that God cannot, and certainly God does, but we don't expect it. But when we go out and pray for a day, whatever other reason we may have, we definitely wish to be with God, to feel his presence and to interact with him in some way. How can we talk about this? There may be times when God "shows up," and we experience his presence and power in a powerful way. These times are up to God.

Most of the time we do not feel a divine surge in prayer. We can be assured of the legitimacy of our prayers without feeling God's conquering presence. Much of the time all we know is that we are trying to pray. To be accurate, all we feel is our faith. We can at least recognize that in prayer in which we feel nothing from God, we can nonetheless feel ourselves believing as we pray. We keep praying because we sense that in some way, when we experience our faith as we pray, we experience God in the very act of our own faith. This sounds fishy, and rightly so, because it may sound as if we are equating our faith with God. Equating human faith with God is a weak theology about a measly god. So in this inquiry we will resist that notion with all of our powers. But what if faith allows us to experience traces of God's presence?

If in our hardest times our faith reaches into the darkness and grasps God, and if somehow we believe that, even though we cannot feel God, and if we can sense our faith grasping God, then perhaps something of faith's grasping is communicated back to us, not as a direct experience of God but as a mediated experience of God whose shape we learn to recognize as the presence of God in personal darkness. We can feel ourselves exercising faith at a time when nothing suggests that we ought to. That is, something is extracting faith out of us. It is our faith, our human faith, and it bears the unique stamp of our particular being, similar to our fingerprints, but we are aware that something is requesting and authorizing our faith at the same time. We cannot feel or sense where our faith is going or who precisely we are embracing, but we feel ourselves exercising faith, and we feel that in some sense it is appropriate. That is, as long as we exercise faith, we lack nothing. In this process we experience our own faith.

Since this is prayer, it is different than simple cognitive faith such as "I believe the Bible is the Word of God." But in asking about experiencing God in prayer, we are not addressing the question of whether God exists; instead we are addressing God as the answer to the question of his existence! This sounds bogus at first. After all, if we pray, then in some sense we are already acknowledging God's existence, but not really. Consider the following: We may enter a crowded room looking for a man named Bill on the recommendation of someone we hardly know, but because Bill *may* exist, and we really need to contact him, we raise our voice and ask for "Bill," not knowing if Bill is there or even if he truly exists. The case of God is different, granted, but if we pray to God hoping that he exists, and though we do not feel God directly, we feel that we have faith in God, and though we cannot say precisely what our faith grasps, we feel that our faith is grasping something, this may be enough to convince us that God exists. However, if we call out to Christ the Son of God for mercy, for the forgiveness of sins, and then we grasp something in faith that responds by grasping us in love—that which grasps us in love transcends our faith. We know that we have need for the forgiveness of sins, and we have never been able to shake that great burden, and we hear that Jesus exists risen from the grave, following a death on the cross to pay for our sins. When we call out to that Jesus, we may not hear or feel anything, but for the first time we feel ourselves having faith, and we feel something change in us. We know that something has happened to our sin. And when we go back and ask again, we feel the same thing happen again. We may not be feeling God directly, but we can feel our faith sensing God and this becomes enough. For "everyone who calls on the name of the Lord shall be saved" (Rom 10:13).

When I pray, something draws faith out of me, and I will pray just because of that. Of course, this raises all kinds of questions about right faith and the right object of faith, but most of us experience God long before we learn of these questions. Later our faith, grasping after God as it does, requires us to seek understanding of God, whom we encounter in faith. As we pray and study and pray and study, our comprehension of what our faith is grasping becomes better defined. But our experience of God through faith is always a mediated kind of knowledge of God. Apart from the glorious experiences of God that come occasionally or once in a long while or once in a lifetime, we exist in our journey through life, with God and with others, on a derived experience of God—the experience of experiencing God while exercising faith and experiencing faith.

Have we entered the region we vowed not to accept, that is, the idea that our faith is God? We may mean this cynically, that what we call "God" is psychological projection of our ego on the universe. Or we may mean this naively, that God is not just everywhere, but God is everywhere and in everything, including in human faith experience. We renounce these options. On what basis? It is undeniable that many people have faith in utterly bizarre gods and spirits, and it is equally undeniable that some souls have made God out to be a special circumstance of themselves. How can we differentiate ourselves from these views? We can differentiate genuine faith and the experience of genuine faith from spurious faith and the experience of spurious faith in comparing the experiences of faith, hope and love.

It cannot be doubted, for instance, that some people cannot differentiate the difference between loving themselves and loving another person. They are so self-centered that they can only love what others can do for them and for the ways others reflect back to them who they think they are. Likewise, it cannot be doubted that some people can never love well. They consistently chose poor objects to love, that is, persons who can only seem to fall in love with addicts or abusers. These people are not wrapped up in themselves. They simply do not know in an internal way how to love someone worth giving their lives to.

Hope works the same way. Some people can only hope for things that directly benefit themselves. And likewise, some people can only seem to hope for lost causes and foolish dreams. As the author of Proverbs says, "Anyone who tills the land will have plenty of bread, but one who follows worthless pursuits will have plenty of poverty" (Prov 28:19).

Alas, people who can only love themselves or can never love well are like those who can only hope for themselves or can never hope for anything realistic. They are unhappy and unhealthy people. But there are those who can distinguish between loving themselves and loving others, and there are those who can make good choices in love, and there are those who can hope for something outside of themselves and who can, with practice, learn to hope for things that actually can occur.

Likewise, though it is true that some people can never have faith in anything but themselves, there are some people who can distinguish between having faith in themselves and having faith in someone outside of themselves, and they can tell the difference between the two. In actual fact, for many people, choosing to exercise faith in someone outside of themselves can be excruciatingly difficult, not because they cannot tell the difference between themselves and whoever they may need to have faith in, that is, a doctor or a minister, but because they can most certainly tell the difference. It is very difficult to give up personal control over our lives in order to trust it to someone else, even someone we can see and argue with, who comes with good references!

Exercising faith is difficult for many reasons, but most of us can differentiate our self from the person or organization or god in whom we propose to have faith. Furthermore, it is the very nature of faith—giving control to an uncertain factor—that we find so difficult. Faith is so problematic that most of us will only exercise it when we have to. That is, we will only have faith in a doctor when we can't sew ourselves up; we will only give our case to a lawyer when we can't fix the problem ourselves. Most of us turn to God and exercise faith when we must. Even if we aren't sure who God is or whether God is listening or not, we can tell when we are exercising faith in God and when we simply trust ourselves to get something done. To put it bluntly, exercising faith in God is sometimes frightening, sometimes unsure, and it always involves a sense of ambiguity beyond the ways and means of everyday life. If prayer is precisely this, if it is placing our lives in God's hand on sheer faith, then we cannot expect this to be pleasant, and we might expect the process to be rather lengthy. I have no doubt that some of us pray longer than others because it takes us longer to give in. We must pray long to experience whether faith in God is really faith in God. We pray long because we cannot run out of questions.

And yet it is precisely those of us most difficult to convince who find that wonderful experiences of God will not, ultimately, suffice to establish deep, personal faith. These seem most likely to be faked. Euphoria is ephemeral. But in the dark night, at the impassable gulf, the leap of faith occurs in the most difficult and arid of circumstances, when we feel our faith go forth and grasp God existing in absolute hiddenness, when we know that faith has hit something true because it is flowing freely, like when electricity surges through a wire in contact with a ground. Prayer can feel like lightning when we feel faith explode out of our soul into silence, nothingness and chaos and hit the ground, the ultimate ground of all existence, when we feel that in our search for a little surety for our sin-sick, wrung-out soul we hit a source of Spirit not merely sufficient for our need but sufficient for the needs of the world. It is as if we looked for redemption of our little soul only to happen upon the redemption of the world, or as if we sought safe passage though the darkness of our little life only to happen upon the light of the world, or as if we sought a little high ground for perspective on our pain, only to happen upon *that than which nothing greater can be conceived.*

And when our faith discovers so much more truth than we ever sought, and our path is illuminated more brightly than our eye can bear, and our sin-sick soul is forgiven of so much more than we could ever deserve, then we realize that what we have come to believe is impossible not to believe, except as an act of rebellion against the will that makes the world and saves the world and demands our all. Our intractable will is reclaimed to desire his will. Then we know that our faith is a gift and a miracle from God. Until the miracle of faith, in which we experience the impossibility of not believing in God, we cannot recognize how pervasive is our sin nor how great is God's forgiveness, nor that the miracle of faith is the transformation of the will.

Seven

The Good Stuff

Words fail us in prayer oftener than anywhere else; and, the Spirit must come
in aid of our infirmity, set out our case to God,
and give to us an unspoken freedom in prayer, the possession of
our central soul, the reality of our inmost personality
in organic contact with His. We are taken up from human speech
to the region of the divine Word, where Word is deed.
We are integrated into the divine consciousness and into the
dual soliloquy Of Father and Son, which is the divine give and take
that upholds the world.
P. T. FORSYTH

The following narrative is the account of a woman's experience of learning to trust God as she spent time in his presence on the beaches ot Cape Cod.

A Personal Narrative

People part with thousands of dollars and sit in countless hours of traffic just to spend a short amount of time at the ocean. I have often thanked God for the blessing of living just a ten-minute drive from a number of beaches, places where seagulls cry out and wheel through tangy sea air, where cold Atlantic water rumbles and whispers, leaving a regular imprint of its presence in newly smoothed sand and freshly loosed seaweed.

Though I've been drawn to the beach by the ocean's faithful ebb and flow, in the midst of its regularity is a constant undercurrent of change, unseen by all but careful observers. The shape of the beach, where and how it meets the water's touch, differs over time. Driftwood, shells and sea glass soften and lose their familiar shape and sharp edges. Even large jetty rocks disintegrate gradually into palm-sized, ovoid stones of gray-veined granite and cool white quartz. Over time, things undergo an extraordinary metamorphosis at the ocean's edge. Almost two years ago, at a time of intense personal crisis, the beaches near where I live became hallowed ground. God met with—and changed—me there through many sessions of long prayer.

From my earliest days growing up in a home that was deeply broken, I had built my identity on lies such as "I am what I look like" and "I am what I do." Without realizing it, however, much of how I viewed myself and presented myself to others, even in the church, didn't change when I became a believer during my college years. I continued subconsciously to invest much of my energy into making myself appear strong, smart, in control and accomplished. Apparently I was fooling "a lot of people a lot of the time," even more recently those to whom I ministered as a pastor's wife. And I was self-deceived, not knowing there was another way of living in Christ. But God, who sees us truly and sometimes deals with us with what Sheldon Vanauken calls "a severe mercy," wanted more for me and broke into my comfortable delusion. How glad I am now that he did!

January is normally a time when my life slows to a pace at which I can hear God more clearly. Two years ago in January, God began to challenge me with questions about how much I truly trusted him, why I lived in so much fear, and whether I would be willing to come out of hiding. Such questions shook me to my core, which was exactly where God purposed to work. I began to perceive a number of "masks" that I routinely wore in my relationships with God and others. Several months later, as God continued to call me out of my "cave," I taught a retreat titled "Free to Be Real: Unmasked by the God Who Sees and Loves Me." God did extraordinary things in the lives of listeners and speaker alike, and I came out of the weekend both exhilarated and exhausted. As I had challenged others to do, I began to remove some of my own masks. What a time of freedom this was but also of raw emotional vulnerability. It was as though someone were tapping at the top of my head and, like a fragile eggshell, a life based on appearances and accomplishment began to fall away. My identity, my perception of who I saw myself to be—based on what I could perform and present to others—was disintegrating. Scary stuff. Who would be left when the masks were gone?

In my journal I wrote at that time, "God has been challenging me about masks. I've taken off some, but without the core of my being/identity being restored, healed, filled—so little inner strength or reserve. My clear call is to stand unmasked before my God—and in that place to be healed, fully known and fully loved. . . . God isn't letting me stay in an unhealthy place but is allowing me to see more of my true state so I will finally come to him for healing, filling, and my identity fully centered in him."

A dear friend, whom the Lord gave me as counselor through this process, encouraged me to carve out some substantial time to come before the Lord and allow the Lord to rebuild me. I readily agreed and found the space for this essential work three mornings a week while my children were both in school.

I drove faithfully to the beach on those first mornings, full of an odd mixture of apprehension and anticipation. Would God really meet with me? Would he be able to pull off the substantial work I so desperately needed done in my "inner (wo)man"?

What was this going to cost me? Would it be worth it? It took very little time arguing with myself to know that God ordained this time, and it was therefore an opportunity I dared not miss.

And how faithful God was. I began each of my three-hour sessions with time spent in silence, quieting my restless heart, choosing to trust that he was for me and wanted to meet with me, asking him to come near and do what only he could do. Much of this time I simply sat in my car, watching the warm sun move over the surface of the beach, seeing amber sea grass dance before a field of azure blue sky. There was comfort, safety, even a measure of healing in just drinking in that beauty, the physical handiwork of the One whom I was asking to create new things in me as well.

I would usually then move to Scripture, letting the Word become a place of conversation between God and me. And God began to speak often and clearly to my heart. Passages such as Paul's exhortation to the Galatians in chapter 5 took on new meaning as God applied his Word to my life: "For freedom Christ has set us free. Stand firm, therefore, and do not submit again to a yoke of slavery." In one of those early times with God my sense was that the Spirit spoke thus: "I have grieved to see you wear the mask of rejection. It is not who I have made you to be. It is not your inheritance. Walk in the depths and power of my love for you, and the mask of rejection will fall from your hand. Let it go. Holding on to it (though it may have become comfortable) will not ease your pain. It has robbed you of so much already. Do not be afraid of the woman underneath the mask. She is less smooth, less placid, less predictable, and she is all mine. Allow yourself to be real. Risk it in me. The freedom is there for you."

After time in prayer over Scripture, I would begin another phase of my extended time with God. Now I would walk, often for an hour or two. In these long beach walks I asked God to accomplish in me what Paul prayed for the Ephesians: "I pray that the God of our Lord Jesus Christ, the Father of glory, may give you a spirit of wisdom and revelation as you come to know him, so that, with the eyes of your heart enlightened, you may know what is the hope to which he has called you, what are the riches of his glorious inheritance among the saints. And what is the immeasurable greatness of his power for us who believe, according to the working of his great power" (Eph 1:17-19).

Three mornings a week for several months I met with the Lord in this way. The times with him were sometimes quiet, sometimes riotously full of his work. But in all of it, how good, how personal our God was in his dealings with me. His Spirit led me through each time, ministering individually to me from a perfect knowledge of my exact need.

God was accomplishing things I knew were real and lasting. In the middle of this season of long prayer, I wrote in my journal, "I've felt a substantial difference in myself since the 'mask work': more core strength, less constant fear. Satan's talons are retracted (there's less for them to sink into, less of a hold on issues of guilt). In a healthy way the Holy Spirit can still convict me of sin, but I'm far less vulnerable to constant attack on 'old business.' I'm doing less wallowing. The Lord has given me a stronger stance in him."

Through my times of long prayer, the Lord did an extraordinary work of rebuilding me from the inside out. He literally repaired the vessel of my personhood and identity. And then, as if that were not enough, he did more. His final and ongoing work was to fill me with more of himself and a growing sense of his tender acceptance of me in Christ.

Because of broken relationships with fathers in my childhood, I had struggled deeply and unknowingly for years to receive my heavenly Father's love. Such a struggle had also kept me from a healthy acceptance of myself and from growing to love the woman God had been bringing to life in Christ. I was, quite simply, empty of the ability to experience God's love personally. One day in long prayer, I sensed the Spirit instructing me in the following way: "Make it a new (and constantly developing) habit to open your heart and arms to me for more of my love. It will be a balm, a healing tonic and the essential gift I have for you now. Be blessed, refreshed and protected by it. Walk in the paths of my love; it is essential for your ministry. . . . Remember, it is the ensign under which you go out into battle. Keep it ever before you. Live, breathe, teach, listen, speak and rest in my great love for you." I knew I needed to receive more of God's love, but how could I move from an intellectual knowledge that God is love to an experience of that love for me?

One particular day God went to "ground zero," calling me to deal with the heart of my relationship with him as my Father. And he chose the ordinary "stuff" of the beach environment where he was to teach me an extraordinary truth. I was well into a long walk down the seven-mile stretch of beach before me when the words of Romans 8:15-16 rang through my heart: "For you did not receive a spirit of slavery to fall back into fear, but you have received a spirit of adoption. When we cry, 'Abba! Father!' it is that very Spirit bearing witness with our spirit that we are children of God." In remembering these words I had a picture of my small, shriveled orphan heart, a heart shrunken in fear and slavery to pleasing others. How much more the Father had for me, and it was already my full inheritance because I was united to Christ by faith!

All of a sudden, on the beach before me shone a tiny, white sea stone, gently rounded by the water's constant caress, gleaming wet in the sun. I stooped to pick it up and have saved it to this day. As I later recorded in my journal, the minuscule stone became for me a clear symbol of "my life—hidden with Christ in God—a tiny and infinitely precious pearl, seen and covered by the Father's love, utterly protected and kept in the deep places of him."

John tells us that God's "perfect love casts out fear," a principle of "spiritual displacement," which I experienced in this season of long prayer with the Lord. As I received more of the Father's love, there was simply less room for fear in my life. In place of my fragile, self-constructed shell, God was strengthening me "in [my] inner being with power through his Spirit." I had become like a tree, the core of which was being "rooted and grounded in love" (Eph 3:16-17).

God's work in me continues. But it was in large part established by the season of long prayer to which he called me. He accomplished extraordinary spiritual surgery in a relatively short amount of time simply by calling me to spend large blocks of time with him and then faithfully meeting me there. Long prayer became the context for developing a deeper trust in God, whose presence I came to recognize and long for. And in a handful of excruciatingly intimate, precious moments borne from the labor of long prayer, God touched and undid twisted parts of me, remade the vessel of my personhood and poured into me his molten, healing love. I will never be the same.

Drafting

Yes, God answers long wandering prayers. In fact, God answers them quite frequently. I expect divine intervention from long wandering prayer. Over and over and again and again God responds. I don't know why. It isn't because I have all that much faith. After all, I just admitted that I struggle sometimes with the existence of God. It isn't that God answers long prayers because they take more time and thus show greater commitment. My commitment to God and prayer is not particularly commendable. All I can suggest is that through the many hours of stubborn importunity, we learn who we are in relation to God's will. Over many hours, importunity and submission become one. It's praying ourselves into the reality of God's will. In long wandering prayer we stop thinking of prayer as sending messages to God; rather we understand prayer as sending ourselves to God in the Spirit of God.

Long prayer instigated by profound heartache ends with heartfelt praise. The original issue, often something of enormous import, *feels* answered when our will desires God more than an answer to the original petition. When the bitter imperative pales compared to the desire to know God—often this is the sign that the prayer has been heard and answered.

In this way, answers stack up so fast that, at the risk of sounding ungrateful, answered prayer seems like normal stuff. I thank God for answered prayer, but more essentially I try to pray past answers to prayer as if they mean very little. Of course God answers prayer.

Is there anyone among you who, if your child asks for a fish, will give a snake instead of a fish? Or if the child asks for an egg, will give a scorpion? If you then, who are evil, know how to give good gifts to your children, how much more will the heavenly Father give the Holy Spirit to those who ask him! (Lk 11:11-13)

Some petitions go back many years and have never been answered to my satisfaction. Perhaps they never will. I just keep praying vehemently, with loud cries and much pleading, expecting that when and if they are ever answered, the answer will seem like normal stuff.

The rare and glorious thing in prayer is the presence of God. Even when prayer is tough and the experience of God is slight and difficult, the presence of God is the issue. In prayer in which faith reaches into darkness and all we can feel is our faith being received and pulled into existence, the presence of God is the issue. But sometimes the presence of God is glorious and wonderful. That's the good stuff.

Describing the experience of the glorious presence of almighty God isn't difficult as long as we don't profess to be able to describe any particular experience as normative. God is one, simple and holy. The truth that we experience God differently says nothing about differences within God. The differences are in us. God condescends to our differences. In the Scriptures diversity of experience with God is the norm. And it is the norm in our lives. We cannot predict what any encounter will be like. I think it is best not to desire a particular type of encounter with God. This is to prejudge what we need and what God wants. When we begin prayer, we only know that we need God. We may know what we intend to pray about, or we may only know that we need to be with God, and the subject will become apparent when we get there. But we cannot predict how the meeting will go. And we must not try to predispose the experience one way or the other. We can fully expect that God will answer our prayers. But we cannot expect how God will meet us in prayer.

Once in a while—it is hard to say how often—we experience God in staggering joy.

In the 1970s Debbie and I took many long trips in a 1965 Volkswagen sedan—the Beetle. Besides many trips up and down the West Coast, we drove the car across the United States at least four times. The car's radio worked infrequently. Driving through the Deep South in days of heavy rains, Debbie bailed water from the floorboard as it collected at our feet. That's the kind of car it was.

On the open highways I loved "drafting trucks." I'd see a semi up ahead, and if I could catch it, I'd pull up, usually less than thirty feet behind it. The truck broke the wind, and more than that, if I could find the right place behind the truck, the air currents coming off the top and sides of the truck would envelop our little metal casing and pull us right along.

You can see the same effect in a fast river, especially while fly-fishing. As the water flows past a large protruding boulder, not only is the water behind the rock rather quiet, but very often water currents form off the main current speeding around the rock toward the back and center of the rock. These offshoot currents curl inward, toward the center of the rock, creating a flow of water upstream. The upstream current is formed by the double foil of water flowing past the rock faster than the regular current, creating a vacuum behind the rock. The upstream currents fill the vacuum. In these currents the fly floats upstream.

Just as the fly floats upstream in the currents behind a big rock, our little car was pulled up the highway caught in the air currents filling in the vacuum behind the big truck. When I drove into the right spot, we could feel the car pulled by the truck. I could let my foot off the gas almost completely. Sometimes it felt like the air currents literally lifted the car up—never off of the pavement—but it certainly elevated the car to some extent. It was fun. But truck drivers didn't like it. They'd shake me off eventually, and we'd have to go back to traveling on our own fuel. It was definitely a dangerous thing to do. Firmly ensconced in middle age, I now discourage the practice. And I suppose it is probably illegal.

When I feel the presence of God, it feels like drafting a big truck. It feels like my prayer goes from being pushed along by a little put-put engine to being pulled by a monster diesel. The reason prayer feels like drafting a truck rather than just getting a bigger engine is that when I feel the presence of God, it feels like I am being pulled by something that I'm close to but can't touch. My feet are still on the ground, but I feel like I am being lifted. My steps feel lighter. I walk faster but much less deliberately. My thinking focuses. Far from being an irrational, ecstatic phenomenon, in this state my rational process leaps forward from point to point, as if I am bounding through a field of high grass on the back of a lion, holding his mane and laughing with glee. No matter what I was praying about, whether I feel an answer or not, all I can do is praise and thank God. I always think best when I am worshiping God.

When the presence of God comes in power, I feel like I can take my foot off the gas. Not only do I not feel my faith at work in these prayers, I never feel physically tired after these experiences. During the prayer, for a little while, my aches and pains disappear. If this is a little foretaste of heaven—I can hardly wait.

It's easy to shy away from mystical experiences for fear of being misled. The devil can pose as a spiritual Mack Truck—just waiting to be drafted for a spiritual adrenaline rush into false thinking. But I have never been lead astray in such experiences. I have never felt tempted during such experiences to turn from my generic, evangelical faith. I have never felt tempted to rationalize sin. I have never heard voices or felt anything unusual at all. Instead during these wild rides, basic, ancient, traditional Christian faith makes vast and deep sense. These times make my doubts seem low-minded and irrational.

Still, genuine risks exist in these experiences. The real risk inherent in these kinds of prayer experiences is precisely where the metaphor between drafting a truck and drafting the Spirit break down. We initiate and control drafting a truck. It takes a certain skill. But there is no control and no skill whatsoever in bringing on these prayer experiences. They happen utterly unpredictably. There is no certain place where they happen. There is no certain frame of mind in which they are more likely to happen. There is no type of prayer, frame of prayer, order of prayer or place of prayer that is more likely than others to initiate these experiences. The reality of these experiences does not negate in the slightest the truth that we pray best when times are hard and prayer is hard, and we don't know if we are getting through or not. There is simply no technology of prayer that can lead to or predict these experiences. But, of course, the risk is that we will fix our desire on these experiences and try to muster them up, or think that if we only had enough faith or the right place or a better frame of mind, then we would experience this more often.

If there is anything about long wandering prayer that leads to these experiences, it is simply the fact that we are there more often. Long wandering prayer is not quality time with God, it is simply long time with God, some of which is very difficult. But if we hang around long enough, something may just happen.

To be completely honest with you, I don't even know if I experience these times with God often, rarely or very often. I don't know how often it happens. I've never kept a prayer journal. I've tried prayer journals a few times, but they last as long as when I take a pocket spiral notebook with me fishing to write down details of the fish I catch. I can't force myself to write about fish when I am catching fish. Later, at home, writing down the details of the day on the stream seems dreadfully boring; I usually watch TV. It's the same thing with prayer. I can't force myself to write about praying when I am praying. And later, at home, it seems impossible to do, so I usually watch TV. So I don't know how often I experience Spirit-drafting prayer. It could be once every four or five years or many times a month. I have no recollection. I just know that when I experience these times, I feel overwhelmingly grateful for the life God has given me: for my family, my church and my community—and I want to go to heaven as soon as possible. At times like these, the difference between answered prayer and unanswered prayer seems pointless.

When I go out to pray long, I expect that God will answer my prayers, but I never expect that God will encounter me in a powerful way. I never expect Spirit-drafting prayer. I never plan it. I never look forward to it. I never hope that it will happen. I never visualize it happening. I don't think about it before I pray or during prayer. As I am driving to a place to pray I never say to myself, "I sure hope I experience God today." I never pray that God will meet me in powerful way. I never ask anyone to pray for me that God will encounter me in a powerful way. My only expectation when I go out to pray is that God will listen and will in some way answer my prayers. And then it just happens. Not all the time, not even most of the time, although I'm not sure of that either. It could be that it happens most of the time. I have no way of knowing.

Conclusion

Perhaps the reason I don't remember how often I have experienced the great presence of God is that looking back over nearly thirty years of long wandering prayer I can only confess that the hardest times of prayer are very good, often the best, and any time with God, under any conditions, is good stuff. There's something powerfully affirming about arguing with God. Like the Canaanite woman forced by Jesus into a theological debate, the act of arguing with Jesus makes us feel smarter and more able—we feel like the image of God. Spiritual doubt can be gruesomely difficult, an act of reaching to God in spiritual darkness, groping for any sense of his reality and presence, and feeling nothing but going after it again and again until we feel like we've inadvertently stuck our finger into a power outlet. No one who has searched for God in this way begrudges God a single moment of spiritual pain during the search for the reality of our resurrected Lord. The few times or the many times we experience God's overwhelming presence—Spirit drafting—or the stone on the shore that metaphorically mediates our hiddenness in God's love—these times fully surpass any pain we may have undergone until the Spirit breaks in. Suffused with the joy of the Spirit in reverse, years of angst take on whole new meanings, testifying to the richly textured sovereignty of God. We see this process in highly condensed form in the prayers of the Bible.

Habakkuk's prophecy is really a dialogue with God. The form is rather simple: Habakkuk complains, God answers, Habakkuk complains, God answers, then Habakkuk confesses his faith. The prophecy is short and contains as many famous verses per line as you'll find anywhere in the Old Testament. Habakkuk begins with bitter complaints:

> O LORD, how long shall I cry for help,
>   and you will not listen?
> Or cry to you "Violence!"
>   and you will not save?
> Why do you make me see wrongdoing
>   and look at trouble?
> Destruction and violence are before me;
>   strife and contention arise.
> So the law becomes slack
>   and justice never prevails.
> The wicked surround the righteous—
>   therefore judgment comes forth perverted. (Hab 1:2-4)

By the end of his dialogue with God, Habakkuk sings a new song of genuine resolution.

> Though the fig tree does not blossom
>   and no fruit is on the vines;
> though the produce of the olive fails
>   and the fields yield no food;
> though the flock is cut off from the fold
>   and there is no herd in the stalls,
> yet I will rejoice in the LORD;
>   I will exult in the God of my salvation.
> GOD, the Lord, is my strength;
>   he makes my feet like the feet of a deer,
> and makes me tread upon the heights.

> To the leader: with stringed instruments. (Hab 3:17-19)

Similar changes occur in some of the Psalms of Lament. In

Psalm 13 David begins:

> How long, O LORD? Will you forget me forever?
>   How long will you hide your face from me?
> How long must I bear pain in my soul,
>   and have sorrow in my heart all day long?
> How long shall my enemy be exalted over me? (Ps 13:1-2)

A few verses later, he declares:

> But I trusted in your steadfast love;
>   my heart shall rejoice in your salvation.
> I will sing to the LORD,
>   because he has dealt bountifully with me. (Ps 13:5-6)

We could multiply the examples many times over. A scriptural prayer begins with horror and ends with praise—in a few verses. The person praying exhibits a dramatic change of mind quicker than we can decide which flavor to put in a fancy coffee.

We want the change of mind, but we can't experience it as quickly as the example in Scripture. So we feel guilty. Or we think it doesn't apply to us. But if we look back over many hours of prayer—the prayers of a whole day, several days of long prayer, or even months or years of long prayer—we can see the changes in our minds that we see in the prayers in Scripture. Are we just very slow? I don't have a problem admitting that. Or are these short prayers artistic compressions of much longer prayers? What if David prayed Psalm 13 over a long night of torment? When he wrote the prayer for corporate worship, could he make the hymn as long as the original prayer? Habakkuk's dialogue with God reads in five minutes. What if Habakkuk prayed these prayers over a month? Or a year?

We see something like this process in chapter 4 of Paul's letter to the Philippians.

> Rejoice in the Lord always; again I will say, Rejoice. Let your gentle-

ness be known to everyone. The Lord is near. Do not worry about anything, but in everything by prayer and supplication with thanksgiving let your requests be made known to God. And the peace of God, which surpasses all understanding, will guard your hearts and your minds in Christ Jesus. (Phil 4:4-7)

We believe it and we want it and we try it, but it doesn't work. But if we look back over many years of rejoicing through hard times, practicing gentleness when we are tempted to be harsh and praying instead of worrying, we can see that we have experienced the peace of God that surpasses all understanding. But it doesn't happen as fast as it seems it ought to happen, and we feel discouraged that we can't get it right in short prayers. However, maybe Paul compresses the process here. Perhaps his advice comes from his victory won over many years of long prayer. We see this possibility a few verses later when he discusses his sense of contentment.

Not that I am referring to being in need; for I have learned to be content with whatever I have. I know what it is to have little, and I know what it is to have plenty. In any and all circumstances I have learned the secret of being well-fed and of going hungry, of having plenty and of being in need. I can do all things through him who strengthens me. (Phil 4:11-13)

Three phrases stick out: "I have learned to be content with whatever I have," "I have learned the secret of being well-fed and of going hungry," and "I can do all things through him who strengthens me." The Greek in the phrase "I have learned to be content with whatever I have" implies that Paul has taught himself to be self-sufficient. The word *autarkēs* means "content" or "self-sufficient." The Greek in the phrase "I have learned the secret of being well-fed and of going hungry" implies that Paul felt that his ability to live peacefully in plenty came by a secret blessing from God. The word *mueō* means "to initiate into the mysteries" and is used only here in the New Testament. The Greek in the phrase "I can do all things through him who strengthens me" implies that Paul believes his contentment comes from an ongoing blessing of power from God. Paul describes his personal contentment as the result of his journey of faith, mystical blessings from God and ongoing spiritual power from the Holy Spirit. The three ways to contentment are by no means inconsistent. We can hardly imagine genuine contentment without all three. We know that we learn the discipline of personal contentment only through the weal and woe of life. Furthermore, we can look back and see that at certain times God has blessed us with experiences—Spirit drafting—which in some sense initiates us into a mode of contentment that we cannot earn, learn or self-effect in anyway. And we know without the slightest doubt that all of our life experiences and all the mystical outpourings devolve to nothing but stories about old times without the Spirit's ongoing strength throughout our life.

Is it possible to imagine Paul knowing the joy of contentment in life unless he followed the advice he gave the Philippians a few sentences earlier in chapter 4 when he tells them,

> Finally, beloved, whatever is true, whatever is honorable, whatever is just, whatever is pure, whatever is pleasing, whatever is commendable, if there is any excellence and if there is anything worthy of praise, think about these things. (Phil 4:8)

We want to rejoice always, we want to stop worrying, and we want to know peace that transcends the ups and downs of life. Can we have it in shorter order than Paul?

Jesus tells us to "consider the lilies." Does he mean a quick look or a mindful meditation? Five minutes or five years? How do we know he doesn't mean five years?

So yes, the mountain lady's slipper is most meaningful in the prayer life of one who knows it well. And it is precisely the one who knows this orchid well that can contemplate *Cyripedium montanum* in absentia, in a jail or an office cubicle. What a moment of contemplation that will provide!

Notes

Orientation to Wandering
[1]"Discursive," in *Oxford English Dictionary on CD-ROM* Ver. 1.13 (Oxford: Oxford University Press, 1994).

Chapter 1: Long Prayer
[1]P. T. Forsyth, *The Soul of Prayer* (London: Epworth, 1916), p. 96.

[2]Jonathan Edwards, *The Works of Jonathan Edwards, Volume I*, revised and corrected by Edward Hickman (1834; reprint, Carlisle, Penn.: Banner of Truth, 1984), p. xlvii.

Chapter 3: Long Wandering Vision
[1]Dietrich Bonhoeffer, *Life Together*, trans. John Doberstein (New York: Harper & Row, 1954), p. 77, emphasis in the original.

[2]J. Behm, *"noéō,"* in *Theological Dictionary of the New Testament*, ed. Gerhard Kittel and Gerhard Friedrich, abr. and trans. Geoffrey Bromiley (Grand Rapids, Mich.: Eerdmans, 1985), p. 639.

[3]Walter Bauer, William Arndt and F. Wilbur Gingrich, "κατανοέω," in *A Greek-English Lexicon of the New Testament and Other Early Christian Literature* (Chicago: University of Chicago Press, 1957), p. 416.

[4]Ibid., pp. 476-77.

[5]Bonhoeffer, *Life Together*, p. 77, emphasis in the original.

Chapter 4: Battering the Heart of God
[1]Dietrich Bonhoeffer, "Bonhoeffer's Lectures on Preaching," in *Bonhoeffer: Worldly Preaching*, ed. Clyde E. Fant (Nashville: Thomas Nelson, 1975), p. 133.

[2]*Webster's Third New International Dictionary of the English Language Unabridged*, ed. Philip Babcock Gove (Springfield, Mass.: Merriam-Web-

ster, 1986), p. 1135.

[3]Ibid.

[4]Forsyth, *Soul of Prayer*, p. 131.

[5]Joseph Fitzmeyer, "The Gospel According to Luke X-XXIV," *Anchor Bible* (Garden City, N.Y.: Doubleday, 1985), p. 1179.

[6]Bonhoeffer, *Life Together*, pp. 45-46, emphasis in the original.

[7]Thomas Goodwin, *Works of Thomas Goodwin: The Work of the Holy Spirit in Our Salvation* (Carlisle, Penn.: Banner of Truth, 1979), p. 147.

[8]Isaac Watts, *Isaac Watts's Guide to Prayer*, abr. and ed. Harry Escott (London: Epworth, 1948), pp. 25-28.

[9]Bonhoeffer, *Life Together*, p. 86.

Chapter 5: Worthless Guilt About Things That Don't Apply

[1]David Hansen, *A Little Handbook on Having a Soul* (Downers Grove, Ill.: InterVarsity Press, 1997), pp. 171-73.

Chapter 6: How Can Something I'm So Bad At Be God's Will for My Life?

[1]Eberhard Juengel, *God as the Mystery of the World*, trans. Darrell Guder (Grand Rapids, Mich.: Eerdmans, 1983), p. 168.

[2]Ibid., p. 192.

[3]Ibid., p. 181.